Wildly You

PERMISSION TO FAIL FORWARD INTO SELF-AWARENESS AND ACCEPTANCE

HEIDI BARKER, L.Ac. DAOM

 AUTHORSUNITE

||| AUTHORSUNITE

Authorsunite.com

ISBNs

Hardcover: 979-8-9850092-0-0
Paperback: 978-1-951503-62-8
Ebook: 978-1-951503-63-5

Dedication

For my daughters. And to all the women that have felt less than, put into boxes, told they have to show up a certain way, or be a certain way. To those that have been invalidated, called 'too' much, or told that they are to be seen and not heard. To those that have not been offered a seat at the table. Permission to be... Wildly YOU!

Table of Contents

Introduction

Welcome, friends. I'd like to invite you into my story and share my experiences in hopes that this book leaves you feeling inspired, entertained and encouraged. My intention is that, in some small way, this book will give you permission to find your way home, back to yourself, and those small parts that may have been forgotten, pushed aside or neglected. In a world rampant with comparison and criticism, it takes sincere effort to deeply know yourself and not only understand, but honor what you want. I think that's why the self-help section in the bookstore, and the life coaching profession has grown so much in the last decade.

We are all craving awareness and an intimate relationship with ourselves, and to have a greater respect and relationship with that whisper inside us all. It takes some practice to feel into your purpose and desires and choose to live in alignment, regardless of the outside world. I am an imperfect person that has had the fortune of some incredible experiences, a healthy dose of right timing, and a wildly adventurous spirit. My desire is that by sharing my story of successes and failures, my vulnerability can be a mirror for you; an invitation to turn inward and reflect and remain open. It is a practice that I strive for and hope we can all support one another along this rewarding journey called life.

Leap of Faith

I'll never forget being 7 years old and sitting in my brother's green '64 Chevy as he drove me to swim practice. My brother is 12 years older than me, so he got the job of towing me around from time to time. "What do you want to do when you grow up?" he asked me. Kind of a big question for anyone, let alone a 7 year old.

"I want to make a difference," I responded. Which seemed to fly out of my mouth with such confidence and ease, it's as if I could feel his question before it was asked.

I'm not 100 percent certain that I knew what the weight of those words really meant at the time. However, I do know that from a very young age, I felt a strong urge to do and be something meaningful – to have an impact on other's lives in a powerful way. I just wasn't exactly sure what that would look like. I mean, like I said, I was only 7 at the time.

So here I am, sharing my story, decades later. For so long I have wanted to do this, but I was held back by the notion that what I had to say wasn't dramatic or impactful enough. I also got stuck in the belief that *'it's not the right time'* and *'I don't have the time.'* And while I do believe in divine timing and not forcing things, there came a point where I had to ask myself: *"how much longer until it will be the 'right' time?"*

So after 7 years of upholding that limiting story, I decided it's like standing on the edge of a cliff; the more you consider all of the possible outcomes, the less likely you are to jump so you're better off just taking a big breath and a leap of faith, and going all in. So here goes my very own leap of faith.

I am confident that within these pages you will find something that you can identify with. Maybe a feeling you have had or an experience that you thought was unique to only you that in some way, might have kept you small or had you feeling that you couldn't or shouldn't (fill in the blank with your own limiting belief/story).

I want this book to give us all permission to be seen, to be heard and to live a truly authentic life. Myself included. And to give you, dear reader, an opportunity to establish the most intimate relationship with yourself. To fully commit to knowing yourself. To explore who you are and what you want to create, as you tap into your individual gifts.

My Parachute Story

I was 29 when I thought about making my first career transition. I had been in the military for six years at this point, and after attending the Naval Academy, it felt like even longer. I had spent time researching so many fields that I thought would be of interest to me like Law School. I loved to debate, but I didn't love research.

And then there was Medical School, but so many doctors I spoke with were disgruntled at how little they actually felt they were able to help their patients. Many felt like they had become slaves to insurance and big pharma, and were left to manage people's symptoms with pills because so few wanted to accept responsibility for their own health. I was eagerly looking for a profession I could fit myself into (and an identity), which is when I stumbled upon a great book called, <u>What Color Is Your Parachute?</u> This book asked me to determine who I was *before* I decided what it was I would do with my life. And a lightbulb turned on.

Think about that for a second. Instead of asking the age-old question of: *What are you going to be when you grow up?* What if we asked things like: *Who are you, and what amazing talent will you share with the world? How will you share that talent, and what do you want that to look like?*

<u>Bottom line:</u> what will allow you to be WILDLY YOU?

This was the beginning of developing an intimate relationship with myself. I was asked to prioritize what I loved and before I could do that, I had to take the time to determine what that actually was in the first place. I had to get incredibly honest about what was truly important to me. And honestly, as exciting as that felt, there were also equal parts discomfort and fear that accompanied this next level of inner knowing.

Up to this point in my life I had made choices seeking achievement, or because someone told me that I couldn't. (Insider tip: don't tell an achiever-type personality that they can't do something!) Other times, my decisions were based on proving myself or, like so many of us, choosing things based on trying to fit in. But this book asked something different of me. This book was saying, *"Hey, Heidi... instead of determining what shape hole to plug yourself into, get clear about your shape and your identity first. Who are you and what do you really want out of life?"* From there, it would be up to me to discover or create an occupation that aligned with the real me. What a frickin' novel concept for a people-pleasing, uber-achiever. '*You mean, I get to decide what I want and how I want it and that's not selfish?*' I thought.

Mind. Blown.

It's so easy these days to live on autopilot. We fall into habits and rituals without even thinking about them. How many times have you gotten from point A to point B and you can't recall the drive? Scary, but true. You grow up, maybe pick a sport to play, go to college, get a degree, start a job, get married, buy a house, get a dog, start a family. Maybe you go to a gym and find yourself parking in the same place every time, and picking the same locker. Basically, you create a daily routine that you follow, which can be great in some ways. The habituation saves us time and allows our brain to contemplate other things while we run the routine on... yep, autopilot. However, a pitfall of routine is that it allows us to operate without conscious awareness, and it can cause us to miss being in the present moment if we're not careful. When we're not present, we might miss a person that could lead to a pivotal life change, or an opportunity that we've been waiting for. Or possibly, something bigger.

Another pitfall could be that we get stuck in routines that don't really serve us any longer, or the goals we are working towards as the current version of ourselves. For example, if I get into the habit of eating ice cream every night before bed because it's what I do to unwind and it's what my family always has done (and uh, because it's delicious), it could be sabotaging my fitness goals and my sleep recovery (I know... an unfortunate truth). But I'm doing it because it's a long time habit, not from an intentional space with conscious awareness - and therein lies the problem. Without developing an intimate relationship with yourself and knowing what you want, you may find yourself following the herd and landing in a pasture that doesn't fulfill you. Without awareness you are asleep at the wheel of your own damn life.

I'm going to paint a real picture of vulnerability and honesty here.

I have failed as much as I have succeeded. And you know what? My failures turned out to be the fertilizer for my future success. I have had to step back frequently and re-evaluate my identity, my purpose and my why (intention). It has not been a linear process. In fact, it has been quite an adventure. The most amazing adventure of Lewis and Clark magnitude. Going into the unknown on a daily basis with a sense of curiosity and a sense of humor has been my guidepost and mantra. Something I invite you to adopt, or at least try on for a bit.

In the pages to follow, I will show you how I have created a unique life that reflects my passions and gifts, and how you can, too. I will share my failings and stumblings along the way, which were necessary to create a more intimate and clear relationship with myself. And I will share how I continue to cultivate awareness and make it a cornerstone in my life.

When I learned to trust my inner guidance, my life transformed in the best way possible. I want this for you, too. I want you to feel so sure of your soul's whispers that ignoring them is no longer an option. My journey thus far has been to get quiet enough to listen and hear these nudges and in doing so, step further into my truth to become wildly me.

Let this book be your permission (if that's what you need) or simply an invitation to tap in, tune in, and reconnect to your heart. And from this place of aligned authenticity, to take the action necessary so that you, too, can become WILDLY YOU.

As you uncover what's been keeping you safe, small, and maybe even stuck, I am inviting you on an adventure into the depths of possibility. It's time to explore your wild parts, and get curious as you open yourself up to the life waiting for you on the other side of courage.

I hope you're ready (or at least willing) because...
Into the wild we go!
xo Heidi

CHAPTER 1

The Space Between Our Ears

"Your imagination is everything, it is the preview of life's coming attractions." – Albert Einstein

The idea of space exploration began in fiction novels written by Jules Verne in 1865 and H.G Wells in 1900. And it was their brilliant imagination that inspired the scientific investigations in the beginning of the 20th century. Their visions and dreams are so commonplace now that any person (with enough money) can buy a ticket and head into outer space, which is amazing! I'm pretty sure Jules and H.G are impressed with their forward-thinking ideas, as they should be. And then there's Elon Musk who has taken it a step further by being an incredible dreamer and manifestor; the true embodiment of Einstein's quote at the top of this chapter.

My 3rd grade teacher was fascinated with space exploration as well. She brought the discussion of space into our social studies class to use it as a parallel to discuss the explorations of Lewis and Clark. It was especially relatable for me at the ripe age of 9 because part of the Lewis and Clark trail goes right through Boise, where I grew up. The trail parallels an area called Lucky Peak Reservoir, a place full of fond memories including many days spent swimming. Or, if I got super lucky, long afternoons spent boating with a friend's family. I was intrigued by the idea of Lewis and Clark and how insanely courageous and adventurous they had to be to venture out into the unknown wilderness. This kind of courage was becoming more common for people in the 80's only now it wasn't by horse and buggy, but space exploration instead. This context made it a hot topic for teachers, posing questions to their students to get their curiosity and adventurous sides revved up.

My 3rd grade teacher took this opportunity to ask our class, "What do you think is the next place for us to discover?" Some of my classmates said the ocean... other galaxies was also a common response, and some even said more places on our own planet, like the jungles or Antarctica. My answer was a little different. "Our brains... you know, the space between our ears and the thoughts we think about ourselves." Pretty deep for a 9 year old; a consistent theme in my life, no doubt, as an introspective deep thinker. But first, a little backstory...

A year before 3rd grade, I discovered this old book written by some seemingly important Russian swimmer. I wish I could remember the title of it because this book was a pivotal read and moment in my young life. It had a picture of a pool on the front and it was blue. For being such an incredibly impactful read, I honestly can't remember much about the overall context, maybe something about swimming to win. Anyway, the section that grabbed my attention and ultimately, changed my life, was the portion on visualization. The general concept was that you could visualize your race and by doing so, you could then perform in the manner that you had mentally rehearsed. My little mind was blown away. I had a moment of profound knowledge that I had stumbled upon a real secret to the universe. *You mean to say I can finally put my overthinking, over-analyzing brain to work for good?* I loved the idea. I had a really vivid and overactive imagination so it made perfect sense to apply it in a productive way. Another way I dealt with my monkey mind was through my interest in music. Aside from swimming, I was also really enraptured by singers, both their talent and what they produced.

I was in the Honor Choir, and I desperately wanted to be a good singer so I would record myself singing onto a blank tape and play it back to work on my pitch. I had a naturally deeper voice so I was put in the alto section of the choir. I was so disappointed by this placement. I don't know how much I'm dating myself here but the song, Borderline by Madonna came out in 1983 and I was struggling to hit those high notes, which was crushing to my little soul. When I sang into that tape player, I was certain I was giving Gloria Estefan a run for her money. But when I played the tape back, reality hit me like a wrecking ball. Here I was, with this awesome tape recorder and very little promise to become the next pop star, so I decided to give my not-so-talented pipes a rest, and try recording visualizations for myself instead. If becoming a top performing artist wasn't going to be in my future, maybe swimming would fill the gap.

Discovering Mind Games

By the age of 6, I was already winning first place medals and trophies in my age group for swimming with records at our local YMCA. Which was cool, but I really wanted to compete on a National level because that's what all the older kids were doing. And truth be told, I was unusually motivated by fancy trophies. So when I found this life-changing swimming book a few years later, I decided to practice the elements of visualization to try to take my game to another level - and it worked!

At the time, I wasn't that strong at breaststroke. Butterfly, Individual Medley and Freestyle were my strengths. So I used this as the perfect opportunity to visualize myself swimming breaststroke and what it might feel like to be really excellent at it. The book suggested incorporating as many senses as possible, so I would imagine the feel of the water on my skin, my body position, my breathing, my turns - all of it as pragmatic as possible. Just weeks after my first attempts at visualization, we had a swim meet in Payette, Idaho and the trophy was absolutely massive, which had my eyes bulging out of my face like the cartoons! It had three tiers of faux brown marbled laminant lined with big green reflective stripes, and a big gold ball with a swimmer perched on top. I had to have it. But in order to take home my age group high point trophy from the meet, I was going to have to win the breaststroke. And as my luck would have it, a new family had just come into town from Alaska with 4 girls who happened to be awesome at breaststroke. The odds were not stacked in my favor, but with sheer determination, and the power of mental rehearsal, you better believe I took that trophy home.

At another meet there was a beautiful purple jewel in the center of the tall gold trophy. Again, my cartoon-bulging eyes were front and center! My mom told me that I had just aged up so it was highly unlikely that I would win the high point trophy. You see, in this particular meet I would have to win the 50 yard freestyle and usually, the longer events were my strength. But I decided to put my mind and heart into it, just like the book said, and I won the 50! And managed to take home that glorious trophy as well, which felt even more exciting because purple is my favorite color.

Moral of the story? What we believe we achieve. Or, another way of saying this, energy follows thought. If I believe that I am capable of something, I am more likely to manifest the outcome. We all are. Which is a pretty incredible superpower that we don't need any special skills for other than our minds! I believe this is, at least in part, the case due to one powerful system - the Reticular Activating System (RAS). "The reticular activating system is - it starts above your spinal cord and it's about two inches long, it's about the width of a pencil, and it's where all your senses come in. Well, except for your smell, which goes into your emotional center of your brain, but the rest of them come in through the RAS and what the RAS does is really connect that subconscious part of our brain with the conscious part of our brain." - Lori Rothstein, Educator.

The RAS comes into play when we decide that purple is our favorite color and all of sudden we see purple cars and purple buildings everywhere. I have experienced the RAS most recently with my daughters who both have red hair. Red hair supposedly occurs in only 1-2% of the population, but now that I have red heads, I see them everywhere.

Do we magically manifest what we think, or are we just more aware that it is existing around us because of the RAS? I think there's a little of both, but no doubt the RAS can be used for good in helping us reign in our thoughts and focus to help us create a desired outcome. Powerful stuff!

In Neuro-Linguistic Programming (NLP), we're taught the importance of focusing on what we want, and not on what we *don't* want. This just further supports RAS. If we focus on what we *don't* want, we're likely to be more aware of things that support that ideology because it is in the field of our RAS. Simple enough.

I believed I was really good at swimming, and that was supported by my family. I received a lot of really good attention as a result of that so that became a lot of my identity as a young child. I developed stories to support my success, and habits as well, which all influenced a positive outcome. Ultimately, I manifested my success in part because of my mindset. But also, because I took wild, messy action on top of all the mental work I had been practicing. And that is the power of the mind.

Success Doesn't Trump Presence

It was extremely important to me to create success for myself because my dad was pretty absent in my life. He was an extremely driven man that achieved incredible things in his lifetime, but that came at a cost - his family. He was born in a small town in Maine and grew up with a tremendous amount of adversity, raised by a mother that ran a boarding house on the railroad for railroading men. I'll never forget my dad sharing the story with me of being just a baby. He was not gaining weight and his mom wanted to take him to the hospital but my grandfather refused and insisted that if it was 'failure to thrive' then it was better to let him go and let nature take its course. "Survival of the fittest," my dad joked as he laughed in a self-deprecating way about it. I could always sense the hurt from him when he shared that story, but he shared it like a badge of honor. My dad was a survivor *and* a thriver.

Luckily, my grandmother snuck my dad to the hospital and discovered he had pyloric stenosis. And after receiving a life saving surgery, my future was secured. Shortly after this event, my grandfather left and my dad was raised by the men on the railroad tracks in his place.

I often refer to my dad as a cockroach, which I mean with the utmost affection and admiration. He is truly the most resilient, driven and optimistic human I have encountered in this life. I don't know if cockroaches are optimistic, but they definitely seem to go after what they want with a zero-fucks attitude. That was my dad. And although he was amazing in so many ways, he wasn't emotionally set up to relate to a young girl or connect with the sensitivity I craved as a child. The best way I knew how to relate to my dad was to achieve and show him how tough I was. But more than success, I desired his presence.

I was fortunate to have a really strong swimming coach growing up, a very big and intimidating man with a booming voice that echoed throughout the YMCA swimming chamber. His name was Pete. The older girls on the swim team took me under their wing and were super sweet to me because I was keeping up and swimming in a lane with people who were 5 years older than me. I remember some of the girls really disliking our coach because he was so demanding, often expecting more out of us than any of us thought was possible - and he used some interesting techniques. I remember getting sprayed with a cold water hose once, while doing 25 yard sprints to 'incentivize me to swim faster. I have to admit, I thought it was strange, but I didn't find it abusive. A lot of the girls complained and wanted to quit but the fact was, we were all getting faster. And my mother loved him. Not surprising that she was a believer of the no pain no gain work ethic. I was improving so much with my swimming, which made all the hard work worth it. It felt really good to be accepted by the older kids on the team who I really wanted to be able to swim with, learn from, and compete with.

All the practices paid off, and I got what I wanted. I was invited to swim at a meet at the University of Idaho, which is about a 12-hour drive from Boise, depending on how fast you're willing to tackle some single lane driving. My mom and my older brother went with me. I remember getting to the meet, looking out at the pool and thinking, 'Wow, these kids are a lot bigger than me!' It was a super scary experience. The warm-up pool was packed with what felt like 20 kids per lane. The pool felt alive and was swarming with people - and I froze. I couldn't do it… I couldn't swim. It all felt too big and intimidating and no amount of mental rehearsal could change that. So I went over to my mom and told her it wasn't going to happen, I wasn't going to get in the water today. I was crying, scared and so disappointed in myself but nothing was going to change my mind. I simply couldn't bring myself to do it. My mom was really amazing and she told me that was okay, but that I had to go over to my coach and tell him why I wasn't able to swim. Facing my coach, someone I looked up to and wanted to prove that I was just as good (or better) than the older kids, was another scary thought. I wanted so badly to impress him, much like my dad. But here I was, telling him that I couldn't get in the water. It was, however, an easier choice than competing that day.

Coach Pete had a lot of kids he was responsible for that day and I don't remember our interaction being of much consequence. I believe he tried to get me to change my mind, but I was steadfast in my commitment to be done for the day. Reflecting back on the incident, I am really grateful that my mom taught me to take ownership of my choices and that she gave me the space to choose in the first place. It was a powerful moment for me, and one I'm grateful for to this day, not being pushed one way or the other. I really value that my mom emphasized that swimming was my choice and she wasn't going to push me into something I didn't want for myself. Little did I know the consequence that would result.

The Drive That Changed Everything

We drove home that morning, arriving unexpectedly, later that evening. The house was locked, which was very unusual, so we walked around the side of the house into the backyard. There was a large sliding door and on the other side was a beautiful bar that my dad had built with railroad memorabilia. It was pretty fantastic. The chairs were old leather railcar chairs, and there was a rail tie bent around the base of the bar where you could rest your feet. He even had the stop light lanterns from rail crossings and a big spotlight, which was the front light from an actual locomotive, that shone onto the bar area.

Just as I came around the corner of the house and arrived at the glass door, I saw my dad sitting in one of the leather railcar chairs at the bar - with his secretary in his lap. I don't remember much from that night other than my mom and dad fought and she and I slept downstairs in a bedroom together. My world was about to be turned upside down.

That was the end of my parents' relationship. My mom and dad had both been previously married and my mom had been adamant about her zero tolerance policy for cheating; it was a deal breaker for her, no matter what. The message I received from my mom after that incident was that the only person you can count on is yourself, which came from her own story and experience in the world. She was another extremely resilient and tough human being equal in mental fortitude to my father, but much harder on herself.

My mother came over from Germany at the end of WWII at the age of 19. She left her fiancé and family behind, and the two girls that were supposed to come with her bailed at the last moment so my mom boarded a ship for Canada all by herself. She arrived not knowing a word of English and made a living as a Candy Striper in a Canadian hospital, and assisted a family as an au pair. I can't even imagine the courage it would require to venture to another country to find a better way of life, completely alone, and unfamiliar with the language. The idea of this is terrifyingly bold. She ultimately learned English by watching Soap Operas on TV. I suppose I get my adventurous gene from my mom, and my tenacity from both of my parents.

The divorce was a really hard time for me. Moving out of my childhood home and leaving the neighborhood that felt safe and familiar was a big shake up. We only moved 6 miles away, but for me it might as well have been 600. So much changed for us. My mom had to get a job and was constantly concerned and stressed. We left a beautiful home with a swimming pool and basketball court for a small three bedroom, one bathroom home - without my dad. I felt the insecurities and aloneness she was experiencing, but it was clear she didn't know how to express it. I didn't feel like I had a safe place to go, emotionally speaking.

I sought out my dad's attention on the weekends by going to his house and trying to connect with him. I got frustrated because watching football or drawing in a conference room while he worked didn't feel like quality time to me. I would come home to my mom in tears. After hearing from me how I didn't feel loved or seen by my dad, then my mom would chastise me for even trying. She couldn't see through her own anger and hurt. She was so angry with my dad, that was obvious and understandable. And she certainly didn't hide any of that from me. Looking back, I can appreciate the situation between my mom and dad and I have no resentment toward them at all. They were doing the best they could with the emotional intelligence they had while going through so much of their own trauma and feelings of betrayal. They were products of their upbringing and the stories they told themselves, and chose to believe, just as we all are. I accept them for who they are and love them for bringing me into this world along with the very precious gifts they gave me, including the way they loved and encouraged me throughout my life.

But as a child, I felt very alone and isolated. I went ahead and picked up the story that the only person I could really count on was myself, and I started to own the story that I couldn't ask for help. Instead, I would do it all on my own. I would be resilient like my parents had modeled for me, and as such, I became ultra-independent and dealt with my pain *alone*… in the pool.

My Happy Place

The pool was such a powerful sanctuary. Without realizing it, I was practicing meditation and breathwork with every workout. In the water, it's just you, your thoughts and a neverending blackline. Since there are no distractions, your thoughts come through loud and clear and I could clearly see and hear what was occupying my head space, and the redundancy of it all. If I was really mad, I would just pound it out in the pool. If I swam really hard and my breathing became more labored, I was able to detach from my thoughts. I would focus on the rhythm I created and I would find myself in this beautiful zone of flow, free from the worries of the world. Without knowing it, I was experiencing the concept that *you are not your thoughts, they are just passing through.* I was not my emotions, they were just passing through. I didn't have the wherewithal to draw that conclusion at the time, but I knew that it felt really good. I experienced a lightness and freeness in the water. It helped that I was also very successful and received a lot of praise and positive attention as a result, too.

My success with swimming started at such an early age. I accumulated a ton of trophies, medals and ribbons. So many, in fact, that I filled up three shelves with trophies and a huge rubbermaid tub with ribbons and medals. Additionally, I was in the Honor Choir and part of the gifted and talented programs at school. I was the epitome of an over-achiever, and I loved it. By all appearances, I was a very successful, happy kid with a super positive outlook on life. I was ready for any challenge that came my way and adopted the mantra, *how hard can it be?* very early on. I would imagine some of that is a result of the impressively resilient DNA I inherited from both of my parents. And I think another large part of it was that I really felt like I had something to prove to my parents, the world and most of all, to myself. I received attention and praise as an over-achiever and that felt good, which had me craving more.

I experienced a lot of positive external validation for things that I could control. So I focused there, and pushed myself as hard as I could to succeed.

Lifeboat Lessons

1. Take time to decide on one thing you want to actualize. It can be a job, a feeling, a relationship. Let your imagination decide. Sit with your hands over your heart, take a few deep breaths and ask yourself: *What am I longing for? What does my heart desire?* Don't overthink it. Trust the first thing that comes up for you.

2. Now take 5 minutes to see yourself manifesting that event or feeling. Incorporate as many senses as possible; sight, smell, taste, touch, and sound. Blow up the picture in your mind and get into it like it's an action movie happening right now. Create your own VR experience in your consciousness.

3. Create an affirmation to support the visualization as if it's already happened and tape the affirmation to your bathroom mirror or your car's dashboard; some place where you will see it more than once a day. Example: *I have my dream job, solutions to my problems come easily, my body is wise, I am grateful.*

4. Consider starting a journal for your dreams. Write down your desires and supporting statements or affirmations.

CHAPTER 2

Little Clydesdale

"To be yourself in a world that is constantly trying to make you something else is the greatest accomplishment" – Ralph Waldo Emerson

Junior High was a super tough transition for me. When my parents divorced, my mom allowed me to continue at the same elementary school so that I could finish sixth grade with the same friends I had shared since kindergarten. Our new home was in a different district, so for seventh grade it meant a whole new group of people. I was thirteen years old, dealing with all the awkwardness that the teenage years bring, and now I had to break into a whole new group of friends; it felt brutal. I get uncomfortable now just remembering how nervous I was about the whole thing. I used to have really unsettling dreams about Junior High, even as recently as a few years ago. I would be wandering the halls, unsure of my classroom. The bell would ring and people that were chatting happily with one another would scurry into their rooms and I would be left outside, distressed about where I was supposed to be and what class I had next. I felt utterly lost and alone without the ability (or maybe it was the lack of *willingness*) to ask anyone for help. Then, I would feel a sense of overwhelming failure. Thoughts of being unable to graduate or having to repeat a class would overcome me. It felt so incredibly stressful. And now that I reflect on that, it must have been a deeply impactful and challenging time for me. Likely more than I realized while it was happening.

This is an important point to discuss. I am so much more aware of the impact of change when I am witnessing it through my kids. Change is challenging for all of us. I have spent a large part of my life shrugging off the fact that change causes emotional distress. My way of coping was to ignore it, pretend everything was fine and move on. That was my ultra-independent, 'I'm tough' way to cope. *Shift happens, deal with it.* This attitude was modeled for me and anything less than 'dealing with it' was weak.

I can see now that when my children experience a lot of change, it creates emotional turmoil, which is totally understandable. For example, when there's a home remodel, coupled with a heavy traveling schedule for their dad and school starting - all at the same time - there will inevitably be some emotional outbursts and meltdowns. Instead of me telling them to 'suck it up,' that it's 'no big deal' and that they're 'being ridiculous,' we pause, talk and hug it out. This acknowledgement and discussion doesn't make us weak, it draws us closer to one another. It gives us a chance to re-evaluate how much we have on our plate and to control the controllables, and let the rest of it go.

Transition of any kind provides us with the invitation to take a moment and pause. There may be an actual grieving process that needs to happen. It's a stop sign that you will pay the price for blowing through instead of honoring the signals. At some point you'll have to reconcile the emotions so you might as well do it now instead of later, when it comes up awkwardly and more forcefully. There is an incredible book called Transitions by William Bridges if you want to dive deeper into the topic.

So back to Junior High… Luckily, I made friends relatively easily. I had a good enough sense of humor and a sense of adventure so other kids wanted to be around me. But even so, I always found it easier to be with the boys. It wasn't because I didn't like traditional 'girl' things. I just liked that the boys were easy to be around, and usually, drama-free. There wasn't any backbiting or much gossiping or choosing sides. We would just hang out and do fun stuff. The guys were great. Even on my YMCA swim team, I would often swim with the boys because they would push me harder and this played to my competitive streak. I had enough drama in my home life and I certainly didn't want any more.

Girls could be really mean, and they seemed to know how to get under people's skin and make others feel *less than*. There's nothing like being excluded or cut out of a group or a party to make you feel unworthy. Exclusion and being ignored, or made to feel unimportant or invisible, is the worst kind of feeling. For whatever reason, girls have a natural knack for doing this to other girls and because of it, other girls don't want to be on the outside looking in so they often get seduced into participating and often, cutting off people that they really care about just to be a part of the 'in' crowd. Admittedly, I danced on the edges of that. In fact, I had a very eclectic group of friends, and was always really interested in different people. I guess if they were more of an outlier, I was intrigued. I liked the misfits, the outcasts, the 'strange' ones. Maybe because I saw myself in all of them, in some capacity.

I was a bit of an outlier myself. My sport wasn't a school sport so even though I was extremely successful at it, no one within my school really understood the sacrifices I was making, or the accomplishments I had achieved. I was getting up twice a week to go to swim practice at 4:30am, an ungodly hour for a teenager (or anyone, really). I would make myself a bowl of instant quaker oats in the locker room after practice, and head to school for a full day only to jump on the public bus after school, and head back downtown to hit the pool for a second session.

It was a lot, but I was committed. And it helped that I loved it, making the long days and tiresome expectations worth it. Mostly, at least.

Comparisonitis

I really enjoyed hanging with the guys, and was so grateful to have so many amazing friends. But I was experiencing a lot of internal turmoil, trying to be a teenager, make my parents proud, have a semblance of normalcy in my social life, and figure things out between practice and school. My girlfriends were all super pretty. Some were cheerleaders, and one even had a modeling contract. I was convinced that everyone was so much more attractive than I was which made me question my enough-ness. My girlfriends were the ones getting asked to the school dances and to 'go steady.' Meanwhile, my guy friends would always talk to me about the girls I spent time with, wondering how they could get close to them. I was living out the 'always a bridesmaid, never the bride' energy early on. Everyone would always tell me how easy I was to talk to, and how easy it was to hang out with me. But somehow, I wasn't ever the girl they wanted to date. I felt totally sidelined in love. And in Junior High, that can be downright torturous.

I had an epic crush on one guy in particular. He would throw me enough attention every once in a while to keep me bated, but inevitably, he'd end up choosing another girl; the track star, the cheerleader. Anyone but Heidi, which made no sense because I was awesome... wasn't I? He even had the audacity to tell me one night that someday I was going to find an amazing guy and he would be incredibly lucky to have me. As I share this with you now, I threw up a little in my mouth at the memory. I am so mad at myself for tolerating that kind of BS and moreover, believing it. I let those experiences give more fuel to the story I'd adopted which said I wasn't good enough. The reality is that I was a unique and strong girl that came off as intimidating. I wasn't just enough, I was *more than* enough.

I was a disciplined and focused kid with super high and rigid moral values. Drinking, drugs and sexual activity were a total no-go in my mind, and I felt very self-righteous over those that chose differently. I had a really clear idea of what was right and wrong and there wasn't much gray at all for me. I was so uptight about it that I condemned a couple of girls for showing up drunk to a party I had in 9th grade. They were girls that I had wanted to be accepted by, but danced on the fringes of their acceptance so it felt kind of good to briefly have the moral upper hand and kick them out of my party. My dad had a really nice house that I had grown up in with a large indoor swimming pool, diving board included, and ample area to celebrate. And somehow, I had convinced him to let me have an end of middle school celebration at his house. It was a good feeling to be that kid that everyone wanted to celebrate with, and have a great time. It was a temporary reprieve from my feeling of unworthiness.

It wasn't long after that I changed my views on imbibing. I mean, everyone was doing it in High School so really, how bad could it be? I decided that as long as I was in control, I would give it a try. Funny enough, the best part about alcohol for me was the *loss of some control*. I thought I was funnier and more accepted when I was drinking with my friends. I was genetically gifted (if that's what you want to call it) with a high tolerance, so that made me a team favorite for drinking games, and I was totally down to try and hold my own with the boys. Even back then, I was always up for a bit of healthy competition. I did a great job of containing my drinking to weekends only, and in a way that none of my performances were affected. I honestly don't think my mom was aware in the least of my intake, either. I was still a great student and athlete, so she had no reason to suspect anything different.

Competitive Advantage

In High School, I was introduced to debate for the first time. It was such an exhilarating experience. Growing up, I was always encouraged to be aware of political issues and history. Given my mom's experience in WWII, we had a lot of discussion about war and what created the impetus for WWII. She would describe the German state to me and how the people were in such a hopeless place, and what a dynamic and charismatic speaker Hitler was. We had some really interesting debates on issues and history, and current policies that were facing the United States. I loved it. I would sit at the table for hours with my mom and her German friends having long controversial conversations. I loved being challenged on my position and point of view, and I got a deep sense of satisfaction in getting others to see another side of the topic. My goal wasn't to change their minds as much as it was to get them to imagine walking in another's shoes; to have tolerance for each other's ideas and opinions. It was fantastic practice for debate. Thus, joining the debate team was right up my alley. So much so that I was spending more time preparing for debates than attending swim practice.

I also had my first real boyfriend, whom I met in my debate class. He was super suave, lived in a really nice place, and had a cool 80's haircut - longer hair on one side, and shaved over the ear on the other. His name was Ian, and everything about him was extra cool. He had really blue eyes and it just so happened that he was way more into me than I was into him. I think I was just so excited that someone actually had the courage to throw some attention my way that I felt the need to reciprocate. He was also a super popular guy so of course I had to be into him because if I wasn't, what would that say about me? This scenario plays out again later in life, so stay tuned for that. All of which was just another reflection of what I felt I needed to do to get the validation I craved to prove that I was worthy (or not). Looking back, I was such a brat to toy with his emotions, something I realized too late. I had no idea what I was really doing, other than letting my hormones lead and embracing my ego's need for momentary satisfaction and approval. None of it malicious, but unconsciously unkind just the same.

Despite being deep into debate and exploring an imbalanced relationship, I was still swimming, although half of what I was doing before. My coach was concerned and as such, let me know that I was trying his patience. So when I got wind of an awesome swim meet coming up at the University of Washington in Seattle, I knew I had to be there to prove I was still one of the top swimmers - and my ego really wanted that exposure. There were going to be some great swimmers that were contending for Division 1 scholarships in swimming. The event was also going to be on ESPN, which was extra exciting. I begged for him to let me go and I promised I would be more committed in my swim practices thus, refocusing my priorities. He agreed to give me a chance.

Just one week out from the Seattle meet, a good friend decided to have a party and I decided to let loose. It was a combination of shots, drinking games and my competitive advantage taking over telling me I had to go bigger and harder than anyone else. It was a night of so many bad decisions. One of my good friends ended up running through the sliding glass door because he didn't realize it was closed. He shattered the whole thing and miraculously, was unharmed. I was so drunk that I spent a large portion of the evening worshipping the porcelain God and hoping I didn't see my toes come up through my mouth. I was full-body wretching with the sounds of a full-blown exorcism. How the neighbors didn't hear our shenanigans and call the cops, I have no idea.

The remarkable part is that, in spite of my night of debauchery and almost certain alcohol poisoning, I went on to have the swim meet of my life the following weekend. I won the 200 butterfly and dropped 14 seconds off of my time. I went into the meet with a 2:12, swam a 2:00 in prelims and a 1:58 in finals that night. It was unreal! I was 2 seconds under the Olympic trial standard. That swim at that meet changed the trajectory of my life. Now, Division 1 schools were interested in me! I felt like I was in a dream. I had visualized what I wanted and here it was, right in front of me! Now what?

I had watched so many older swimmers graduate high school and go on to great swimming schools like UC Berkeley, Texas, University of Florida, and graduate with meaningless degrees. If you agreed to sign on and swim for a college, they owned you. Your priority would be to swim really fast for them and, oh yeah, get an education in your spare time. And if you were injured in those four years, you risked losing your scholarship. I watched all of this very closely and I saw how so many swimmers would come back to Boise and flounder as they transitioned from athlete to oftentimes, a big question mark. I knew I couldn't afford to do that. I didn't have a back-up plan or a family that could help me pay my bills while I figured things out. I felt an immense sense of pressure to create some security for myself and now that I was in High School, time was running out.

Peace, Love and Military, Man

I had unconsciously adopted and owned the story that, 'money is scarce, I need to work hard and get a job to provide for myself,' due to it being a huge focal point since my parents divorce. It wasn't that we didn't have enough, it was just that my mom *felt like* it was never enough. I felt the constant burden she carried and I wanted to make sure I never felt that way, personally. Maybe I could even (eventually) lift some of that burden for her.

Enter: the United States Naval Academy.

When they reached out to me in the Fall of my senior year of high school, I knew nothing about the military. I did know that if I got injured, my school would still be paid for, I would owe them *nothing* financially, and I would have a guaranteed paying job immediately upon graduation. My mom was a huge fan of the idea. Much of her family had served in the German military, and she respected and appreciated the American soldiers that came into Germany to end the war. She also happened to love discipline. She often mentioned that she wished she had the opportunities that I had, and how incredibly fortunate I was, a story that continued floating around in my brain.

I was a hippie and a free spirit growing up. I liked to challenge conventional thoughts and push against dogma or systems that didn't seem efficient or necessary. So of course, friends that knew me challenged me by saying things like, "there's no way you'll survive at a military academy!" But all I heard was a challenge, which lit a fire under my ass to actually consider going. I had an opportunity to prove a bunch of people wrong, and to prove to myself that I could do something most people weren't willing to do while making my mom proud in one fell swoop. My next thought: Where do I sign?

I was always up for a challenge, especially one that showed others what was possible - and what I was capable of. The easiest way to get me to do something back then was to tell me that you didn't think I could. Even when I got to the pool for the first time, I remember someone mentioning that I was small and stocky so I should try diving instead of swimming because I didn't have the height or body to be a good swimmer. It was all I needed to hear to push myself from the very start. I had an absolute addiction to proving people wrong. I was also addicted to proving myself, *to myself.* I could drink more, lift more, swim farther, push harder, do more, you name it. If I could go hard enough, maybe at some point I would *be* enough.

The Myth of Enoughness

There's so much pain and effort in that struggle and strife. I wish I could go back to the little girl version of myself and hold her tight. I would tell her how absolutely awesome she was (and still is) and that she never had to prove shit to anybody. She was enough then, and I am enough now. And so are you, the incredible soul reading this now. Just by waking up and breathing every day, that alone signifies your abundant enoughness. Your individual make-up is one-of-a-kind uniqueness; that is your DNA, your fingerprint. You will never ever exist again like you do in this moment right now - in this lifetime, or beyond. There is not another you in this entire world and it is your life's purpose to embody your individuality, and live authentically. The *proving* was taken care of during your divine creation, when it became known that you would exist as YOU.

What a load that would have eliminated from my shoulders to know that I was exactly where I was supposed to be, doing exactly what I was supposed to be doing just by *being,* and that I didn't actually have anything to prove at all - to myself, or anyone else.

Unfortunately, for far too long, I believed I wasn't enough, and I owned this story, specifically around my looks.

I was a very strong little girl. My dad used to call me his 'Little Clydesdale.' And while Clydesdale's are strong, majestic creatures, it's not the descriptor you're looking for as a representation of your dad's admiration or affection, especially as a young girl. My dad was an amazing man, but the poor guy definitely struggled to relate to me, his daughter, who happened to be... a girl! He was a boxer and a fighter so of course he thought that calling me by the name of a strong *horse* was an excellent compliment. I can remember him asking me to stand tall and make fists while pushing myself down toward the ground to make myself heavy. Then he would challenge his friends to try and lift me. I became part of their evening entertainment. "Come on, try to lift my solid, stocky daughter; I'm sure this won't have any negative future consequences." Not his words, but looking back, this definitely created some repercussions. As a result of these antics, and the close relationship he had with my older brother from my mom's first marriage, I was convinced that my dad had wished I'd been born a boy.

To add insult to injury, my mom would often tell me that I wasn't a 'skinny girl' and I never would be. This happened as a result of a shopping trip where I couldn't get my thighs and butt into a single pair of jeans. I would have to buy something two sizes too big in the waist to accommodate my lower half, and then have them completely altered and hemmed just to add more attention to how misshapen I apparently was in the fashion world. I get it. My mom was just being honest about how she saw my body which she saw as strong and healthy. But all I heard was, "you're big, heavy, and you'll never be skinny," and instead of feeling empowered, I felt less than.

When it comes to body image, it really is tricky as a parent. I try to tell my girls all the amazing stuff they can do with their bodies instead of focusing on their shapes or sizes. Regardless of my best efforts, I am sure they'll still find things they feel I could've handled better. But I'm doing my best to stay open and flexible, and provide them with all the love possible as we both navigate the confusion that is parenthood (and childhood).

Back in the 80's, having a muscular body with thick thighs as a girl wasn't emulated anywhere in the media. It was all about the elusive 'thigh gap' and for me to achieve one of those, I would literally have to do a squat. Or cut off pieces of my body, which was clearly not an option. I love that nowadays we are working harder as a society not to be defined as much by the number on the scale. There are so many examples of physically strong girls and girls with bigger bodies. The strong female athletes, politicians, and change-makers taking the world stage are all different sizes, colors and ethnicities showing that your color, shape or culture doesn't determine your fate. It's a beautiful thing. I desperately wish that I had not let any person's beliefs become my own without scrutiny. I wish I knew then that the numbers were, and are, meaningless. And that it's always been up to me to know my depth and own my authenticity.

If I could go back in time and change one more thing it would be to eradicate my people-pleasing tendencies. Growing up, it was definitely the path of least resistance. In the classroom, the teachers loved me because I was so accommodating and compliant. It was also the easiest way to keep my mom happy and off my back. My mom was very rigid and had extremely high expectations for which I am (in retrospect) so grateful. However, when I managed to say something that was offensive to her, disrespectful or troublesome, the punishment I often received was in the form of being dismissed or ignored. She would get really upset with me, for sure. But then she would give me a heavy dose of the cold shoulder, which I think was just her way of dealing with her own suppressed anger. She seemed to bottle it up inside so as to not completely lose it on me, thus shutting me out until she felt like she was capable of re-engaging. And when she would finally re-engage, it was as if nothing had transpired and everything went back to normal, which was confusing and uncomfortable for me, and created a feeling of being on eggshells at times. Because of this, I learned to do and say whatever it took to avoid that feeling of ostracization.

I can't imagine what it was like for her to have all the demands she did on her plate. She was absolutely doing the best she could with what she had, and she was an awesome mom! But ultimately, being ignored or shut out is an awful feeling. It compounded my feelings of unworthiness and aloneness, which I was already struggling with.

I didn't even really have the wherewithal to process all of my emotional turmoil at the time. Without the ability to self reflect and see the situation in its totality for what it was, I internalized a lot of it and decided I needed to 'do/be better.' For me, this is where the pool, once again, became my savior and safe haven. I decided that I could go back to that sanctuary and *smash out my mad* in the water, and find my zone where everything felt better. That's how I got my dopamine hit. Fortunately, I chose to take out my frustrations on my body to the point of exhaustion where I felt the dopamine rush by way of physical movement, instead of consuming copious amounts of drugs or alcohol day in and out.

Getting into my body got me out of my head, and it's still my go-to method for self-soothing. One would likely think that was the better choice. However, years and decades of horrible self-talk and self-inflicted over-exercising to the point of abuse can be just as destructive. However, I think when dosed appropriately, it can be extremely effective.

Lifeboat Lessons

1. Practice a progressive relaxation visualization. In this visualization, start by relaxing from your head and face gradually moving through your body, down to your feet. Imagine a sense of warmth and heaviness moving throughout your body. Each exhale is an opportunity to let go, and each inhale brings spaciousness.

2. Then imagine using your mind's eye to look from within at the living miracle that is you. With your eyes closed, do a scan and take time to marvel at each structure as if you were seeing it for the first time. Marvel at the miracle of it all. For example: when you arrive at your lungs, be in complete awe of the magnificence of all they do without you even having to think about it. How they exchange CO_2 for oxygen and bring life into the body. Take time to get curious about these amazing structures within you all the way to the cellular level. Initiate an intimate conversation with your body through this focused body scan and consider your anatomy, with awe and wonder as if you are witnessing a miracle. Because you are! Fall in love with your cells, and feel gratitude for the inner workings of your being. Contemplate the processes that take place inside of you that make you *you,* and allow your body to function so powerfully and vibrantly. You are a miracle, and that is no small feat.

3. **Bonus:** Be in awe of your brain and it's thoughts, imagination and ability to compute and solve...

31

and your heart's ability to feel and sense. From this finite awareness you can cultivate a greater awareness of when you are in your mind and thoughts, or in your heart and feelings.

CHAPTER 3

Swimming to Safety

"When you're different, sometimes you don't see the millions of people who accept you for what you are. All you notice is the person who doesn't." – Jodi Picoult

Water is such a special medium. It is one of the most powerful and patient elements. The ocean or the river, over time, can wear away stone. Nothing can stand in its way; it even has the power to extinguish fire. We come into this world in water, after all. And the water for me, as a child and now, as an adult, is still a very quiet and sacred place that's always felt like coming home.

I guess it makes sense that it became my sanctuary as a kid as I managed the tough dynamic between my parents. My current assessment of my parents is that my mom and dad were two incredible survivors that were deeply wounded from their upbringing. They were most likely attracted to each other because of their similarities, including their traumas. My dad was impressed by my mother's determination and strength, and she was enamored with his intellect and ideas. It's so interesting that what they most admired about each other is also what they ultimately criticized the most about one another. They brought their wounds into their budding relationship and instead of finding a way to heal, their past became amplified and toxic in their attempt to find and hold onto love.

My dad would complain about how my mom had impossible standards and nothing was ever good enough or done the right way. Ultimately, he never felt as though anything he did was enough. A sentiment which I could relate to at times.

My mom's biggest criticism about my dad was that he was a dreamer and seemed to constantly need external validation, so much so that he often trusted people that were looking to take advantage of him. She would get annoyed by how much attention he needed as a way to stroke his ego and feel 'enough.' For the record, I think my mom desired similar amounts of stroking and she was simply projecting her own shortcomings. At least that's how I've come to see it all these years later.

Either way, they were both correct.

Dueling Dynamics

I have a tremendous amount of empathy for both my parents. My mom's first relationship, when she came over from Germany, was so naïve and unfulfilling.

She met an Italian man that had also immigrated from Europe, so they had that in common. They met in Canada and quickly fell in love and got married. He was a man about town, and had a very hard time remaining faithful to his wife. He saw marriage and family as his duty, but that didn't inherently imply monogamy. While my mom, on the other hand, is a fiercely loyal person. Probably something they should have discussed before they had 4 kids together, but they were also living in very different times. Even when I discuss this topic with my mom now, 68 years later, she reminds me emphatically, that I can't even imagine women's circumstances back then. She didn't have the same opportunities and choices that I have now. She was also in a country where she had no family - completely on her own, of which marriage provided a physical and emotional sense of security. Family was something she wanted, and also just something you did as a woman. In her mind, it became her sense of purpose. My mom, married with 4 babies to look after, worked at the hospital, so she was stretched really thin. She would hurry home and make dinner for the family and when her husband would come home, he'd eat and head out for the evening with his friends. Meanwhile, my mom was responsible for putting the kids to bed and preparing for the next day. She would hear stories from other nurses about her husband's infidelities during his nightly outings, which of course hurt her. But she didn't know what to do. She didn't have an exit plan, so she dealt with it the best she could, and made the most of what became a shitty situation.

In the 60's, before my mom and dad had met, my mom went to Australia with her then husband and their 4 kids. Her first husband was part of a group of railroading men that were going to lay extensive railroad tracks through the outback of Australia. Can you imagine taking four children, all under the age of 10 to the outback with very minimal resources and support to live for a couple of years? My mom is the one that should be writing a book! Her story is unreal.

Enter: my dad.

My dad happened to be working on the same project, which is how they met. And in the heat of the Australian outback, a romance was born. My dad was in Australia with his then wife and young son, and my mom was struggling, very unhappy in her current marriage. Infidelity certainly doesn't justify infidelity, but it's clearly not that simple. And with all the context provided, you can see how this likely wasn't the most stable foundation for a future between the two of them.

It's worth mentioning an interesting fact about the work my dad and my mom's first husband were doing. "In 1968, 137 men laboring in the heat and sun of West Australia obliterated a world record for laying the most track in a single day. They laid 7 kilometers of track in 11 hours and 40 minutes beating the previous record of 4.6 kilometers set in 1962. In all, the crew laid more than 400 kilometers of track between Mt. Newman and Port Hedland in just 9 months." There was no such thing as 'safety workers' or rest. These men had a deep sense of camaraderie, and an insane work ethic. They were driven beyond belief.

It's no surprise that with the endurance of both my mother and my father, my siblings and I were destined to have some pretty intense and driven DNA.

Their upbringing and struggles also paint a pretty clear picture of the need for validation and the deep wounds of lack of worthiness and value. Neither had a problem rising to the occasion, and found a way to do 'whatever it takes.' They didn't have a back-up plan or support system so it was up to them to persevere and create something meaningful.

My mom ultimately ended up with my dad (surprise!) after their romantic connection in Australia. As a result, my mom moved to Boise, Idaho to be with my dad, along with the two youngest children from her previous marriage. I was born in 1973. And a happy blended family we became. That is, until their marriage fell apart many years later.

Guppy No More

My mom had learned to swim growing up in Germany and was on the swim team in her younger to teenage years. The time she spent in Australia included a lot of time in the ocean. It was a place of comfort for her, just as it was for me. She introduced me to swimming at an early age because we were fortunate enough to have an indoor swimming pool. The house my dad built was a source of contempt with my mom because she felt he was living beyond their means and not managing their money well. It was an awesome house, and a great place to grow up as a kid.

My mom was a part of the master's swim team at the YMCA and she enrolled me in swim lessons. I started out as a guppy and worked my way up to shark. The obvious progression from there was to join the swim team at the ripe ol' age of 6. Funny enough, I was actually terrified to put my head under the water until I was 5 years old. Because of this, washing my hair was a constant battle between my mom and I up to that point. So parents, if your kids don't take to water initially, don't make too much out of it. It could just be a phase, like so many we face throughout our lives.

The first day of swim practice was extremely intimidating, but some older swimmers were there to welcome me onto the pool deck as my tears subsided and I felt welcomed by my new pool family. I won a first and second place ribbon at my first swim meet and from there, I was hooked.

The swim team was a really special place for me, sharing a love for the water with a group of incredible people, and athletes. The people I gravitated towards pushed themselves to be the best they could be in the water, which inspired me. They were driven and disciplined, and I felt right at home in their presence. There were a lot of unique individuals on the team and everyone showed up in swimsuits just as they were, which was refreshing. I don't remember ever feeling any judgement or awkwardness, only support and a sense of friendly competition. I was acknowledged for my abilities and accepted and appreciated for my hard work. It's so interesting that we all were around each other in such little clothing, yet I never felt self conscious or judgemental of others shapes or appearances. I guess that's why it felt so good. It was a very safe, innocent environment where I could just disappear into the water, basking in the comfort of the songs I sang in my head as I swam. It was fun and empowering.

On this particular team, there were other outliers and loners that I was able to identify with. It was obvious that a few of us were marching to the beat of our own drum, which I loved. And we bonded through our sport, identifying as swimmers. It was the closest I had ever felt to fitting in.

My mom was incredibly supportive of my swimming. She swam masters herself, and got certified as a stroke and turn judge so she had something to do with every swim meet we attended - and we attended a lot of meets! My poor mom, the amount of travel and time dedicated to a swimmer is unreal. The weekend meets are literally allllll weekend. They start Friday night, and continue until Sunday evening. And often, they were not in Boise, so that also meant commuting, getting a hotel and paying for meals out. It's a massive sacrifice for a parent, as any swimming family will attest. There is no way I could have had the success I did without my mom's selflessness and sacrifices to get me to practices and swim meets. I am so grateful she saw my potential, and supported my aspirations the way she did.

My dad had no involvement in this part of my life at all, even before the divorce. He never took me to a swim practice or attended my meets growing up. Yet, whenever I met people he worked with, they would tell me how he bragged about my accomplishments and was over the top proud of me. I was often shocked by how much they knew about what I had accomplished because I wasn't even certain my dad knew about all that I was up to. There was so much animosity between my dad and mom, so they rarely spoke after their split. She was, understandably, so angry and hurt by him, and I think it hurt her even more to see how uninvolved he was in my life. I can also imagine that it was nearly impossible for him to feel comfortable being involved, even if he wanted to. I am not giving him an out, but it truly did seem like a tough situation for anyone, let alone a parent who'd royally fucked up and wasn't up for admitting any of his wrong doing. He felt like all he was good for anymore was money to help support me, which was largely true, but also self-created by his act of infidelity. My mom was angry at how emotionally checked out my dad was with me, and how could he not be? Being emotionally available seemed like a foreign concept to him, and she didn't have the capacity to help him in that area.

All in all, their relationship was destined for failure. As a child, the disconnection from my dad made me feel alone and I adopted the story that my dad simply didn't care.

Daddy's Trophy

And then, in the 5th grade, I proved that story true. After qualifying for the YMCA Nationals, which was a huge deal at such a young age, I went to my dad seeking financial support. The meet would be held in Fort Lauderdale, Florida over a 5-7 day stretch, which meant it would be a big expense. Because my dad traveled so much, he had a ton of airline miles so my mom suggested that I ask him if he'd let me use some of those miles for a plane ticket. But when I approached my dad with the request, he became super defensive and claimed that he already gave my mom child support, and it should come out of there. Meanwhile, he had just bought his new girlfriend a fancy convertible. It was all very confusing and angering as a child. I stamped my foot down shouting, "Fine, I'll never ask you for another thing as long as I live." And that was that.

My dad was making plenty of money and seemed happy to lavish his girlfriend with anything she wanted, but he couldn't find it in his heart to buy his daughter a plane ticket for a very important swim meet in Florida? Anger, hurt, disappointment, devastation. The validation of the story that *I didn't matter*, and *he didn't care* became very real for me. I was nothing more than a trophy to my dad, at least that's how I felt at the time. He bragged about me, sure. But ultimately, he wanted nothing beyond the surface and then didn't even want to support me beyond the minimal child support he already begrudgingly gave my mom. That one left a mark and I carried it with me for quite a while.

When I returned home to my mom's house after the altercation with my dad, she only compounded the strife. She doubled down, agreeing to the story that I was nothing more than a trophy to my dad. He "obviously didn't care," followed by stating what an uncaring person he was. In my mom's defense, she was a straightforward woman and in her eyes, she was being honest. And that's exactly who she was - a brutally honest woman, with absolutely no filter and if you couldn't handle it, well, that was your problem. The war and her upbringing didn't give her the luxury of exerting much empathy, or emotional intelligence. This was made apparent in times like this where my soul needed comfort, but my ego felt the need to step in and protect my heart due to the lack of compassion I received.

Achievements Masking Truth

I did such a great job of burying all the discomfort and trudging forward. Anyone from High School would have described me as a very confident, self-assured leader. I was awesome at being on cruise control when it came to achievement. I was part of the gifted and talented programs in grade school while I was swimming. I had a closet full of trophies and medals that only continued to grow. I had at least one, if not several records in every age group I swam in at the YMCA. But every new achievement was nothing more than a brief dopamine fix, then I was on to the next. I can see now how it was all extrinsic validation. Having a growth mindset was an unknown concept for me at the time, and I continued to be externally driven as to quiet something lingering inside.

It wasn't that long ago that my niece, Amanda was visiting and mentioned that she knew someone who broke several of my collegiate swimming records. She sent me a list of all the records and accomplishments I had earned throughout my college career, which was a crazy moment for me. First, I was disoriented thinking, *is this real? Did I really do that?* I felt like I was reading a CV of someone I had never met before. My next thought being, *wow, all of those high altitude adventures did a number on your brain, sister.* The reality of it though, was that I didn't remember most of it. There were a few big highlights thrown in there, but most of what she'd shared I had completely forgotten about. So I decided to google myself and gave myself permission to celebrate the shit out of every accomplishment I'd had along the way. And with that,

I started to cry. *What the fuck, Heidi! You never even stopped for one second to celebrate!*

Maybe you can relate to this. I mean, how often do you actually celebrate yourself and, taking it a step further, make celebration a regular practice?

I do have a picture of myself after my last swim of my college career. My mom was there in the stands giving me a hug and I remembered that I had started sobbing uncontrollably, yet I didn't know why. It was like a sneeze. I didn't know where it came from, I just unhinged the pressure and it flowed like the Ganges. No more stuffing or holding back, I felt everything all at once.

That was a good moment.

Hungry For Acceptance

That wasn't the only way this 'not good enough' story showed up in my young life, though. It also showed up in college via a control issue with food.

Swimming was my identity and now in college, it became the foundation of my self-worth. After a pretty grueling season where my coach had me swimming the 400 IM, 500 Free and Mile at every meet, I missed a National standard cut by a very minimal amount. His comment to me was, "well, you did gain a bit of weight over Christmas break... maybe that was part of it." It was a really benign comment, yet as we know, words matter. In retrospect I should've been honest and told him that I was smoked and feeling overtrained. Instead, the people-pleasing, up-for-any-challenge, 'I'll show you' version of myself just said, "okay, noted."

I then put myself on a massively calorie-restricted diet. I was swimming 8-10k meters some days, and I was eating under 1,000 calories a day. Writing this now, it doesn't even seem humanly possible. I kept a food log and became so strict that I wouldn't even let myself chew gum because it had a whopping *5 calories* in it. I was so proud of myself for my discipline and restraint and in the beginning, it paid off beautifully. I was getting all sorts of compliments for how lean I was, which felt great. As you can likely imagine, our military uniforms were about as flattering as a mumu so the only way they looked good was if you were rail thin. The pants were the equivalent of your average pair of dockers, and the shirts were stiff polyester short sleeve button downs. Which meant, the skinnier I became, the more flattering the uniform looked. That was, until it became baggy and hung off me like a clothes hanger.

I was dating a super dreamy guy who played on the water polo team. He was two years older than me. Tall, blonde, and tan, he was an adonis from California - your classic surfer type. I was shocked by the fact that he actually took any interest in me, thinking it was some kind of a joke. His dorm room was down the hall from mine during my sophomore year and it was like kismet. I remember being out in the hall working on a poster of some sort as he walked by and stepped over me with a melodic, "hi." I looked up and blushed and immediately thought, *no way... this guy is so out of my league.* At the time we met, he was still kind of involved with his high school girlfriend and I recall noticing that he had a picture of her on his desk. She was a very attractive blonde girl from

California, and the comparison and not-good-enough feelings compounded. Blaine and I eventually began a romantic relationship and he was really concerned with my condition. He didn't understand why I would do something like this to myself. We were about a year into dating when the discussion with my swim coach happened, and I started starving myself.

It wasn't just Blaine that was frustrated, either. My roommates were angry with me too. People started pushing me away because they didn't understand why I would do something so destructive to myself, and they didn't know how to talk with me about it. I was able to swim okay for a little while, but once I dropped 20-30 pounds and was below 10% body fat (which is super low, especially for a woman), my swimming started to decline. I was undefeated through my college career up to this point and I remember coming in 3rd or 4th in an inter-collegiate meet in the 500, feeling confused. Wasn't I doing the right thing by watching my weight, and keeping up my fitness routine? I couldn't even get through a practice without jumping into the divers hot tub to warm up. My body fat was so low. It was obvious that something was really wrong. I felt more alone than I ever had and now I was also mildly addicted to this new behavior. Finally, I was skinny and fitting into 'the' jeans and fitting into the golden mold that society had been promoting for happiness, fulfillment and acceptance. Yet here I was, isolated, lonely, and misunderstood. Nothing felt right, which left me feeling extremely conflicted.

Blaine talked me into getting some outside support. Our relationship was suffering and he thought it would help. And I certainly couldn't risk losing him, so I agreed. I couldn't go within the Naval Academy for help, otherwise I would likely be kicked out and determined 'unfit psychologically' for service and I could not risk that. Therapy also cost money, which I didn't have a lot of, and I didn't really have anyone to ask for financial support. So Blaine suggested that I reach out to my dad. This meant I had to go back on my word from 5th grade, when I refused to ask for his help ever again. And although it felt like a blow to my ego, I swallowed my pride. After all, it was easier to do that than risk losing Blaine.

Blaine and I drove to Pittsburgh where my dad was working and living, and after a vulnerable (and awkward) conversation, he agreed to support me by paying for some sessions. He didn't really understand what was going on. But he trusted Blaine and they seemed to connect, so Blaine spoke on my behalf. My dad was remarried to a woman almost half his age who seemed to be very attracted to my dad's financial resources. After Blaine and my dad spoke, I overheard my dad talking to his wife about the situation. He said that he never really understood me, and thought I was a cold person. I couldn't believe what I was hearing. I just wanted to get out of that house. Every time I reached out or set myself up to attempt to connect with my dad, it would end up going painfully sideways. It was hard growing up, feeling disconnected from my dad, emotionally at least. I didn't want to align with my mom's point of view, but growing up, he made it hard not to.

Help Is On The Way

When I finally went to see a therapist, it wasn't exactly what I had hoped for. The first took one look at me and with confusion on his face stated, "Eating disorder? You aren't even that skinny… are you sure you aren't just looking for attention?" I was shocked and left that session, speechless. I remember getting up and telling the man I didn't think we were a good fit. I was like, *Jesus, even when I'm literally starving myself and nothing but skin and bones, this jerk is telling me I'm still a big girl.* I wanted to scream. I had dropped 40 pounds by this point and went from a healthy size 10 pant, to a size 0. To question me from the perspective of attention-seeking felt offensive.

After that session, while in a workout, I felt like I almost lost consciousness as I was swimming. I made it to the end of the lane and pulled myself out of the water. As I sat on the edge of the pool I was flooded with thoughts, and a bit of self-judgement. *What the fuck? Am I killing myself? Am I ruining my reproductive system in the process of all of this, too?* It was a super scary come-to-Jesus reckoning because the truth was, it was never about self destruction or ending my life. It was about control and proving people wrong. In the process, I became enamored with the fasting feeling and the compliments. Doing my best to fit into the skinny girl jeans and fit a certain type of body image was taking its toll. Sure, I was now 'fitting in' to the societal expectations, but I had lost myself in the quest for outside acceptance.

Thankfully, I was able to find a second therapist, who was great. Unfortunately, I lied to her a lot in the beginning because I was scared of losing control as I added calories back in and saw my body changing. The jeans I had worked so hard to get into no longer fit. I didn't recognize my shape. The healing process was a long journey and as great as the therapist was, it was blatantly obvious that true, lasting change had to start with me. I had to realize that I was not happy or feeling fulfilled and the choices I was making were not serving me. It was an opportunity to hear the calling of my heart for the first time in a long time. *What are you doing, Heidi? What do YOU want?* I became acutely aware of the illusion of happiness, and how I'd correlated my external circumstances (and body) to achieving that. It was then that I began journaling again to get in touch with my inner voice and my heart's longings.

Lifeboat Lessons

1. Pick up a journal and a pen (or use your phone), and write down and reflect on the things you have put off celebrating. Make a list and give yourself permission to celebrate the heck out of your accomplishments, big and small alike. Going forward, note daily accomplishments and get in the habit of celebrating yourself in ways that spark joy for no other reason than *because you can.*

2. Go back through your life and reflect on times you stayed small or didn't celebrate, without judgement. Find a picture of yourself during that

stage of your life and take a moment to celebrate yourself. Imagine showering that version of you with accolades and joy.

CHAPTER 4

"If You Were A Horse, We Would Shoot You"

"The real difficulty is to overcome how you think about yourself." – Maya Angelou

You might think that because of all the swimming I'd been brought up with that I would have realized before I joined the Navy that I get seasick. I did throw up on plane rides as a young kid when we flew overseas, but it never occurred to me that I might not do well on the ocean. The water was my safe-haven, after all; my true home.

Turns out I don't just get 'kind of' seasick, but I can even throw up during a 5 mile ocean swim. (How's that for an #overachiever!) Found that one out during a winter training trip in Florida. It also turns out, you can puke and just keep swimming. You know that viking ship ride at the fair that slowly rises until it's suspended on one end, and then drops down and through until it's on the complete other end? Just thinking about that ride now has my stomach in knots. It's my kryptonite, no doubt.

Before my second year at the Naval Academy, I got really seasick on a sailing cruise from Annapolis to Nova Scotia, which was ironic because I was in charge of cooking and feeding our crew. Being below deck, smelling chili while your stomach is doing somersaults isn't a recipe for success. I also got really seasick on an amphibious assault ship later in my Academy summer cruise time and as a result, I was found 'not physically qualified' to serve in a line capacity. The abbreviated term is NPQ for 'unrestricted line service.' That meant I had to choose my service designation from restricted line service. I had to choose from the Supply Corps, which is the logistics side of the Navy, Intelligence and Cryptology. I had a wonderful family that looked after me at the Naval Academy and through that relationship, I was mentored by an Admiral in the Supply Corps. I looked up to him and respected his council very much. I thought that was for sure the best path to take and if the Naval Career didn't work out, the Supply Corps curriculum would set me up nicely to transition into business in the civilian world.

I graduated from Annapolis in the summer of 1996. Supply School didn't start until the fall of 1996. Since I minored in Spanish, I was offered a sweet deal to study in Salamanca, Spain for a few weeks and then work in the Embassy in Madrid until Supply School began in Athens, Georgia. What an incredible summer that was. I was a little hurt, initially, because I really wanted Blaine, who was still my boyfriend at the time, to visit me while I was abroad so that we could make some special memories. It wasn't going to be possible with the commitments he had to the Navy, which left me feeling like less of a priority. Looking back, I definitely looked for ways to validate that story because of my own insecurities I had within the relationship. I chose to confirm the 'you're not a priority' story because he was unable to share that really important adventure with me. It was not true.

Una Maravillosa Aventura

I had the most wonderful time in Salamanca, experiencing Spain with some friends from the Academy. We went to school during the day, but partied our pants off well into the early morning every night, dancing and getting to know the local culture. After four years of regimented swim training and the rigors of the Naval Academy, this was pure freedom. And we didn't waste one ounce of it! We traveled to nearby towns, sampled all of the local fare and lived like kings (and queens).

When classes ended in Salamanca, I went by myself to Madrid to work temporary active duty in the Defense Attaché Offices (DAO). It was initially a bit overwhelming. The hustle and bustle of Madrid left me feeling small and scared. I didn't know anyone, and the language wasn't my native tongue so I was really out of my element. It made me further appreciate the courage it must have taken for my mom to leave her country all by herself at such a young age. Here I was with support, and although my adventure was temporary, I could feel the fear penetrating the deepest parts of my spirit. Thankfully, my fear quickly changed to joy as I met the people I got to work with in the office. One of the men in the office was an avid salsa dancer and introduced me to the nightlife and heart beat of Madrid. I fell in love with the energy and the passion of the people. Every day felt like an adventure as I learned more of the city's secrets. The culture of the people and the food made me feel right at home.

That experience spoiled me. I had the beat and the vibe of the city down so quickly that I became the DAO's city expert for incoming dignitaries and guests. I was the personal escort for the flamenco shows, culinary experiences and bull fights, or whatever the desired city tour was for that person or event. I couldn't even believe that this was my reality. It was a dream. When the call came for me to report to Supply Corps School, I begged to extend my stay. I had proved myself as an asset to the DAO so they supported me in fighting for me to stay, but Big Navy refused saying, "No way... she has orders and she has to come back." So a dear friend of mine from high school met me in Madrid and we took two weeks to travel through Europe before I had to report to school.

We had the most incredible adventures traveling from Spain through the South of France into Switzerland and down into Italy to meet up with my extended family. We had no idea where we were staying and relied on intuition and sheer luck to get us from point A to B. We had the no-plan-plan. I could write a whole other book about the adventures George and I had in the summer of 1996. Suffice it to say, it's a miracle that we survived! We absolutely had guardian angels watching over us. We stumbled into the most serendipitous meetings with people and the right time, right place type of experiences that wove an aspect of magic into our entire journey. We were in the flow of our adventure and 'living in the now,' Eckhart Tolle style, without knowing what we were doing. It was the absolute power of presence and flow by dumb luck. Pure magic.

When our adventures came to an end, I arrived in Southern Italy to meet up with my extended family. I had no idea how I was going to get back to the United States or make it to Supply Corps School. I figured I would just get a military flight out of Naples, Italy. But as it turned out, they weren't very predictable or regular. I hopped on a flight down to Sardinia and luckily, caught a flight back to Baltimore, Washington. Once I landed in Baltimore, I was too young to rent a car and had no way to get back to Annapolis to check in before my leave ended. Luckily, I bumped into an officer that was headed back up that way and he offered to give me a ride. The luck and timing of that entire chain of events still blows my mind. The no-plan-plan was more perfect than anything I could have orchestrated for myself.

This is where the joy came screeching to a halt and the real stuff came crashing in.

Lost

I reported to Supply Corps School in Athens, Georgia and had to get back into the classroom and sit and learn all day long. The hard part was that none of the stuff I was learning really felt exciting to me. I ended up struggling in one class in particular, which was taught by a woman that graduated from the Naval Academy several years before me. She kept me after class and was embarrassed by the fact I was doing so poorly. The topic wasn't difficult and I could understand her frustration with me. How could someone with my pedigree be failing in her classroom? She was mildly disgusted and she was not shy about letting me know that I was a 'disappointment' to her. It was tough love, the model she learned coming up through the military, and she was just paying it forward. I felt so incredibly lost.

Before school even started, I had met a guy. Sweaty from a long mountain bike ride, I came into my new apartment as he was doing a tour with the property manager. She mentioned that I had just moved in. "Hi," was all I said, and never thought much about it. The following week, the same guy happened to be in my class. He had apparently asked the property manager about me after being sold on the aparentment's location. He told me long after meeting that it had been something to the effect of, love at first sight. His name was Paul. He had graduated from Pittsburgh, got a commission in the Navy and was now in my class at Supply Corps School.

Paul crushed school. He had been a business major so all of the classes we were getting were the equivalent of dumbed down versions of accounting and supply chain management that he had already received. He gladly took me under his wing and coached me through as much as I was willing to apply myself. The woman that had previously lectured me adored Paul, and I think she ended up giving me a little extra grace because she knew he was really fond of me. Everyone loved Paul. He had great charisma and presence and when he was in uniform, he bore a striking resemblance to Tom Cruise. He didn't just turn heads, sometimes they noticeably snapped.

I was relatively oblivious to Paul's feelings for me at first. My attention was captured by his generosity in tutoring me and providing extra help. He found out that I was a swimmer and asked me if I could give him some tips to improve his stroke technique. Turns out, it was all a ploy to spend more time with me. I didn't mind at all, having no clue about his deeper feelings for me. He had a tremendous amount of empathy for all I had experienced prior to meeting him and was a really great listener. Come to find out, we had encountered similar childhood challenges and we both really enjoyed being active, so we connected with ease. At this point I was still in a relationship with Blaine. I wasn't looking for anything and was super naïve to Paul's advances. I thought, 'this guy is so incredibly kind and helpful and he's great company.' I was beyond grateful to have such a good friend.

Once again, I retreated into the water to cope with my frustrations with my classwork. I exposed myself to a bunch of different religions and even attended services. But no matter what I tried, I found my spiritual connection in the water and nature. I had a longing to belong and it was when I went for a long run, bike ride or swim that I felt the contentment I sought. I could find it while watching a sunset or going for a hike as well, adventures in which Paul was happy to join me for, and over time, we grew closer.

It was a really nice distraction to explore these experiences with Paul and the friends we made at school. Our cohort became a little family. We would eat together and go out together. There were about 25 of us in total and a group of about 10 of us became super tight. I had two male roommates from the Naval Academy that were in my cohort and Paul lived right above us with two roommates from other colleges. We had formed a great little group. I was personally struggling though. I had a long distance relationship that didn't feel secure, and I was facing a career that I wasn't sure excited me. I didn't know what I wanted, but I knew that a lot of what I was feeling didn't feel right. I just couldn't put my finger on the specifics.

Paul was very eager for our relationship to move forward, and I, a recovering people-pleaser, struggled with boundaries. I knew I needed to resolve things with Blaine, but I also liked Paul and didn't want to hurt his feelings either. I didn't manage the situation well at all. I remember feeling so sick about what to do and how it was going to make them both feel. I didn't think much about what I wanted or what would make me happy. I wanted to make sure neither one of them got hurt but in the process of neglecting myself and my truth, I ended up hurting them both anyway. I wish I had understood the concept of 'what is in my highest and best is ultimately in the other's highest and best.' I might have saved us all a ton of heartache.

I ended up agreeing with Blaine that we were too far apart and that we should take a break from one another. I spent more time with Paul as a result and began to explore my feelings in that relationship. Supply Corps School was only 6 months long so as it wrapped up, we all received orders to different ships. I received orders to an Aircraft Carrier that was being built in Newport News, Virginia. The carrier would then be stationed in Norfolk, Virginia for 3 months. After those 3 months it would go on a 6 month deployment around the world and end up in San Diego, California. Paul received orders to a destroyer, also out of San Diego, California. I was feeling alright about all of it. He was not. He told me that he wanted to marry me and I freaked out. I told him I thought we should see other people during this forced separation and "see what happens." The whole thing felt too forced to me. Something was not fluid and it didn't feel right. Again, I couldn't put my finger on it, but the discomfort was definitely present.

Everyone in our class thought we were so perfect together. They even did a comical skit with him as Tom Cruise and me as Kelly McGillis from the movie, <u>Top Gun</u>. I felt like I was letting him down, but I knew I wasn't in the same place that he was and the only way I knew to manage it was to ask for space. In retrospect, this would have been a great place to pause and consider what I really wanted and why. But I was afraid of losing him and I took on the belief that the discomfort I felt had something to do with me (my fault). I thought that if we just took some time apart, I could work on myself and maybe that would help me get to the place he was already at regarding our relationship and any potential future together.

Get Me Off This Ship

"I'll take orders to any place in the country but Norfolk, Virginia." Those were my words back when I was in school in Annapolis and I was about to eat them. I reported for the John C Stennis CVN 74, the newest aircraft carrier at the time. Another overwhelming experience walking up to this behemoth ship tied to the pier. I still have nightmares about reporting to a ship and getting lost within the bowels of the ship. It took me a couple of weeks to learn my way around the thing. I started small. First, it was getting from my state room, where I slept, to the wardroom, where we ate. And I expanded out from there. Kind of like my experience in Madrid or any time I have been scared. You just have to take that first step. Within a few weeks, I had it all dialed.

My first job was to be the ship's store officer. I was in charge of about 50 sailors, two ship's stores that are like small 7-11's, the ship's laundry, the soda machines, and all the store rooms required to support the operation of those spaces. No big deal (sigh). Luckily, I had a very experienced Master Chief Petty Officer, which is the most senior enlisted rank, who was determined to see me succeed. I think the first day I reported aboard, with my blonde ponytail and workout gear, he rolled his eyes.

My first order of business was to get my division in tip-top shape. I knew that we would all do a better job, and have better attitudes if we felt great! I led physical training most days before our working day started. I was not going to have anyone in my division fail the military's physical readiness test. A lot of the guys and gals hated me for it initially, but after a few months, they were all feeling the benefits. So much so that they were disappointed when we had to skip it due to the ship's requirements. The Master Chief eventually changed his first impression of me, which was a real bonus. I was open to learning all he wanted to teach me so we did just fine. The job part was great and I loved the people that worked for me. I had a strong desire to take care of them and mentor those that were open to it. I saw so much unrealized potential in my crew and got excited about helping them see it in themselves.

Being a young 23 year old on a ship of 5,000 people, where only a tiny fraction are women, is not a sweet deal. I had no idea what I was getting myself into. When I came aboard, women were still not allowed in combat roles so all of the aviation squadrons aboard the carrier were made up of men; the officer's contingency aboard was 95% men. I have no issue working with or being surrounded by men. In fact, being around males had largely been my preference growing up. This was different though. Now, I was living in a city that was going to be stuck out in the middle of the ocean for 6 months with a bunch of men. And it got weird.

I started working out in baggy clothes because I felt people staring at me in the gym, or as I ran around the hangar bay. It got uncomfortable enough that I chose to workout late at night when the gym was mostly empty. One day, as I was getting my lunch, I had a senior officer sniff my hair so strongly that I'm sure he collected a strand or two in his nose before commenting, "your hair smells so amazing, is that apple scented shampoo?" In fact, it was. But seriously, what the heck, creeper? And that was just the tip of the iceberg. As the deployment went on, things got worse. When I discussed my concerns with my female roommate, who was 12 years my senior, she told me that I did shake my hips a lot when I walked and maybe I was causing some of the extra attention. Are you kidding me? I have an athletic body and a bigger butt, it's just my physical makeup! And now I have to worry about how I walk in these combat boots and hideous tan docker pants?

The Admiral on the ship made some inappropriate advances and when I talked to my boss about it he told me to *just* 'avoid him.' *Um, I'm sorry, but are we not all confined to this floating piece of metal in the middle of the ocean, together? How do you suppose I avoid him? Jump overboard?* I felt abandoned by my chain of command so I asked for help, which was already a difficult task. And the answer I got? "Deal with it." The woman who was supposed to be my ally told me that some of it was probably my fault because of the way I walked. I felt defeated.

I had no support and was damned if I did, damned if I didn't. I had to walk an impossible line, but watch how I walked that line because you know, it might be 'too sexy' or 'too' whatever else. How was I supposed to make sure I fit in with my male cohorts, while making sure I did nothing to unconsciously create temptation? And if any of them were incapable of controlling themselves, also making sure not to do whatever I was unconsciously doing that allowed for their lack of self control in the first place. Fuck that! It made no sense. Yet it was my responsibility, once again, to keep it all together and adopt my old belief that I must 'do it on my own.'

Competitive Edge

Six insanely long months later, we arrived in San Diego, CA. I was negotiating my next set of orders when I asked to be the Supply Officer for SEAL Team One. I wanted to go there because I could be in charge of the Supply Team and I could get back to working out. I missed the physical escape and I knew I could at least PT with the guys and that would be a part of my work day without being frowned upon. I was told by the Navy that it wasn't a 'career enhancing job' and that I shouldn't pursue it. But I didn't listen. I wanted to go, and this time, I was making the choice for myself.

Once I got to the Team, it was an opportunity to prove myself and subsequently, my worth. There are currently no female SEALs (the combat exclusion law was lifted 5 years ago, allowing women to fill combat roles). And at that time, there were very few in support roles. I was entering the territory of the ultimate fraternity. Could I rise to a bigger challenge to prove my worth after that diminishing aircraft carrier tour? I was about to find out.

My first day at the Team, I rolled in on my Fat Boy Harley Davidson. I completed a swim/run with the guys, and I think I came in second or third. I beat all of the team on the swim, and they all used fins (I didn't). I was determined to send the message that I could hang and I wasn't going to take any shit. The Executive Officer of the Team loved it because he figured it would inspire the guys to work harder and get in shape. I had my armor on tight from my previous carrier tour, and no one would be able to penetrate it this time.

Shortly into my time at the Team, I was asked to be on the Military's Competitive Pentathlon team. What a great deal to workout and compete as part of my job. During the training, on one of the obstacle courses, I jumped down from 5 feet. Upon landing, I twisted to turn around a pole, and ruptured my ACL, bruised my femur and tore my meniscus. It was excruciating. I went over to the SEAL Team Sports Clinic and after reading the MRI I'll never forget the words of the therapist, "If you were a horse, we would shoot you."

What did that even mean? Was my body damaged beyond repair? This could not be happening. I was an athlete and I defined myself by my physical aptitude and strength. As I hobbled out of there, I decided that this guy didn't know what he was talking about and that somehow, I would find a different solution. I was legitimately distraught with my knee injury when a Naval Academy classmate of mine, that I had been training with, offered up an acupuncturist that had helped him with some joint stuff. The acupuncturist was a very accomplished martial arts fighter, world class black belt and I felt like he might be able to relate. Honestly, I was desperate and willing to try anything.

Turns out my knee Injury was the greatest thing that ever happened to me. That acupuncturist changed my life. Not only did he get the swelling out of my knee and help get my muscles firing again, he taught me how to strengthen parts of my body that were weak, leaving me vulnerable to future injury. He advised me on nutrition to reduce inflammation and promote recovery. And he helped me connect more deeply with my body. I noticed that I started sleeping better, I was losing weight, and my energy also improved! Overall, I was feeling great. So much so that I was able to compete a few months later with the Pentathlon Team in Sweden. It was nothing short of a miracle.

Iron(wo)man

I was feeling so good when I got back from Sweden that I signed up for an Ironman Triathlon that was going to be held 4 months later. A couple of guys from the SEAL Teams did it as well, and I had the fastest time. My ego was so pleased. Someone approached me and suggested that I actually train to compete in Ironman distances, professionally. But that wasn't my goal. I was simply out to show myself that I could do it.

I continued to get acupuncture weekly. I was learning so much about getting quiet and listening to my body and feeling its response to self care and recovery. I was paying attention to my body in a whole new way, and noticing how it was reacting to this type of treatment. It was at this same time that I found yoga. In this stillness I began to feel a sense of relief. It wasn't just physical, either. Sometimes I would start to cry or laugh; the emotions would pour out of me like a leaky faucet. My body had so much to say, and this provided a medium for me to get quiet enough to really listen. I was finally truly beginning to create an intimate relationship with myself.

I wanted to learn this language of self awareness and connection. *Who am I really?* I wondered. My exploration of self care was initiated out of desperation to sustain my addiction to move and validate my identity. But it opened up a world of intimate connection with myself that became addictive in a very nourishing way. I was initiating healing that was so much deeper than my skin, muscles or tendons. I began to get glimpses of how we are so profoundly interconnected. After my first taste, my appetite for learning more became insatiable. I began reading all the Buddhist and Taoist texts I could get my hands on. I felt like a whole universe of knowing and remembering was unfolding for me, and it felt tremendous. My body, mind and spirit were saying, "Yes, yes, yes! This is it!"

Lifeboat Lessons

1. Close your eyes and imagine you are holding a dandelion puff in your fingers. See the dandelion puff in your mind's eye, with its big fluffy seeds. Imagine that each seed represents an interaction from your day; a person, a worry, or a to do item. All of the day's events, happenings and thoughts in your head are represented by seeds on the puff.

2. Take a huge breath and blow all of the seeds to the wind. Imagine the seeds all floating into the wind. You can let it all go and trust that anything no longer serving you is being discarded, carefully handled by the universe.

Note: this is a great exercise to end the day with so that you can go to bed with a clear head, setting yourself up for a deeper, more restful sleep.

CHAPTER 5

The Gift of Claire

"And above all, watch with glittering eyes the whole world around you because the greatest secrets are always hidden in the most unlikely places. Those who don't believe in magic will never find it." – Ronald Dahl

There are literal magical moments in our lives. The universe is a web of enchanted synchronicities that often get dismissed as coincidences. I do not believe, however, that coincidences are just due to 'random' chance, which is why I have become such an advocate of meditation and cultivating awareness. I believe you have to be present to see the magic. To quote Ferris Bueller, "Life moves pretty fast. If you don't stop and look around once in a while, you could miss it."

One of those moments for me happened to be on the first day I showed up to train with the Pentathlon team. I was invited to a party that same night with all of the team members, which I was excited about. Just as I walked into the house, I was introduced to a guy that grabbed my attention, quite intensely. It was such a strong and instant physical attraction that it was almost like remembering, a coming home of sorts. And I could tell that he felt the same way. We all ended up going dancing downtown where I danced the night away with this guy, and we had the greatest time. There was no denying that we had smoldering chemistry.

Paul and I were living together at the time, and he had been working late that night so he couldn't join us. I came home afterwards feeling confused and a little distressed that I had experienced such a strong and instant connection with someone else; someone that wasn't Paul. But instead of facing it and getting curious as to what might be underneath it all, I decided to just ignore it and focus on training. This guy was also in a relationship, so really, it was harmless and kinda pointless anyway. At least that's what I told myself.

It was the year 2000, and the Pentathlon competition was being held in Sweden. Paul really wanted to come to support me, but it was a pretty significant expense so we decided it wasn't likely.

Shortly before our departure, the whole Pentathlon team, along with significant others, decided to go to Las Vegas to decompress and build some camaraderie. Just as we arrived, standing there on the infamous Las Vegas strip, seagull poop dropped out of the sky and landed squarely on Paul's foot. He handled it really well, convinced that it was a good luck charm. We all laughed at his sense of humor and how well he dealt with the whole disgusting event. I never gave it much thought over the course of the weekend. On the last day, as I was checking out of the hotel, Paul ran over to a slot machine to throw in one last quarter. He won $1,200, which serendipitously, was enough to buy the ticket to Sweden. Was it coincidence, or fate?

Nama... Stay with Paul?

Heading to the competition venue in Sweden, one of the competitors who was traveling with his wife asked me how long Paul and I had been dating. "Something like 4 years," was my response. "Why aren't you married?" he continued. "Oh, we are just happy the way we are. We haven't felt the need to force anything," I replied. Meanwhile, I was completely unaware that Paul had an engagement ring burning a hole in his pocket. At the end of the competition we had planned a few days to explore Sweden on our own and apparently he had it all planned out. He'd already found a really sweet spot to propose and when he did, I said yes.

Regardless of my response, I was still feeling so confused about our relationship and the chance encounter I'd had with another competitor on my team. How was it possible to have such strong feelings for someone else, whom I'd only just met, while simultaneously agreeing to marry a man I'd known for years? Understandably, I felt a little disconnected from Paul as my mind struggled to make sense of everything I was feeling. My mind was saying *yes*, but my heart was saying *I don't think so*. I did know that Paul loved me very much and he was a very kind and supportive man. We had a connection, no doubt about that. But on the other hand, I didn't feel secure in our relationship, which was in part due to what felt like Paul's wandering eye and partly something I couldn't put my finger on. I couldn't help but feel like he was always searching for something (or someone) that I wasn't, which was reflected back to me when I noticed my teammate through the lens of lust. I kept talking myself out of my feelings.

Paul often told me that he thought he would marry the 'girl next door' type. And whatever that meant, it didn't feel like it described me in the least. We had also spent a lot of time apart since graduating from school in Athens in 1996. I had hurt him by wanting to see other people back then but when I arrived back in San Diego, we both happened to be single and he started coming around more. I was lonely, coming off the Aircraft Carrier tour, and was open to companionship. We just couldn't seem to let each other go. If for nothing else, I really appreciated his friendship, even if I didn't feel a deep romantic chemistry. I'm certain that my lack of commitment didn't leave him feeling very secure, either. It was an extremely confusing and painful time for me. I felt like such a bad person for being unable, and possibly unwilling, to give Paul my full level of attention and commitment. But I didn't have the courage to follow my heart and I didn't feel like I had a safe shore, no matter what I chose. He was the one constant in my life that I knew and who knew me… and he was willing to let me back in again. That had to count for something… right?

During this same time, I had been so impacted by the healing opportunity with my knee and the acupuncturist I had worked with, I could not stop thinking about it. So much was in flux. I felt an intense amount of internal turmoil, which is also when I really dove deep into yoga and meditation to find some answers.

I started working with a yogi that gave me yoga and pranayama practices to follow. I was also journaling my feelings daily. I was working so hard to find my compass, meanwhile feeling terrible about the pain I was causing others. Just 6 months after Paul's proposal, I met with him and made the courageous decision to give him back the ring. I told him I could not marry him with all of the intense uncertainty I was feeling. And expressed that I needed time to myself to find clarity, which I was praying for daily, along with asking for guidance.

In 2002, my tour with SEAL Team One was up, and I was heading to Mechanicsburg, Pennsylvania for an Information Technology Internship. Paul just so happened to have taken orders out to Mechanicsburg, Pennsylvania as well. Our plan had been to try to be in the same city once we were engaged. In the military, you determine your orders about a year before you execute them. Now, since calling off our engagement, our same-city orders made things somewhat awkward.

The offer for this internship was a great stepping stone, as it allowed me to get a bit of extra education in an area that was rapidly expanding, and set me up really well for future promotions and experience. But I was not doing it for any of the right reasons. I had no interest in Information Technology, it was simply an opportunity to achieve and improve my resume, which I thought would catapult me forward towards success and ultimately, clarity and happiness. My siblings were all very successful in their endeavors and I wanted to be impressive and successful, too. I identified as a successful, driven and impressive individual, yet I found myself stuck in the tricky wheel of comparison, seeking external validation and recognition through my decisions. And as fate, or convenience would have it, Paul and I started hanging out again. I loved his company. And he always knew just what I needed to feel comforted and cared for. He was my best friend, which at times felt confusing to navigate.

Confronting Truths

I was still very dedicated to my yoga practice and journaling in Mechanicsburg. And I had an aha moment while I was on the phone with the guy I had met on that Pentathlon team. You know, the one with the crazy chemistry.

As I laid on the floor of my kitchen, phone in hand, he mentioned that I was so great with success in so many areas of my life, but it seemed like I just couldn't get the relationship piece together. I became pretty defensive because I felt like he was a shit show in that department as well and had no room to criticize - but he was absolutely right. He asked me what I was doing in Mechanicsburg and what I really wanted to be doing. I told him that I wanted to have a job where I felt like I made a difference. The little girl who sat in her brother's Chevy pickup truck 20 years earlier was utterly clear about one thing: I needed to feel like I was having a positive impact in some way; to help better people's lives, including my own. I also needed to see the fruits of my labor. I couldn't just be a cog in this massive bureaucratic machine and *hope* that I would have an impact. I also needed to have enough money to be comfortable, but I didn't need excess. I wanted to have time and flexibility more than money.

I also needed adventure and change. I told him that I wanted to run my own show and be my own boss. "Good luck with that," he laughed. "How are you going to manage that?" I wasn't sure, but I knew that was what mattered to me. While everything else in my life felt foggy, that desire was abundantly clear. The calling of service was coming through - and it was really freaking loud!

I had recently come across the book, <u>What Color is Your Parachute,</u> a book all about figuring out what you wanted out of life, including your core values and interests. It's basically a guide to find your internal compass, to learn to listen to what you yearn for and create a career that supports that. Essentially, exactly what I'd been searching for. Reading this book was such a pivotal moment for me and I realized that instead of trying to figure out where I fit in, I needed to figure out who I was and then create a profession that fulfilled me.

I eagerly listed out what made me feel happy and complete. These items are still true to this day, just a bit more refined and clear. My purpose, or my 'why' then was *to inspire others with my fearless nature and experiences so they could show up as the most authentic and powerful versions of themselves.* My 'why' has now been sharpened to *service, growth and empowerment of myself and others.* Less flowery, but the essence remains similar. That's the power of uncovering your core values and your 'why.' Once you know these things, you can look back on your life and see the common thread that's woven throughout all of your experiences. I was able to fulfill my core values in the military with the people I served. I loved mentoring and inspiring the people around me. I knew it wasn't possible for me to continue to focus solely on that as I progressed in the military, making it easier to recognize my jumping off point.

Now that I am a mom and in a completely different phase of my life, I have traded *achievement* for *experiences* and precious moments. Connection fills my bank account instead of accolades.

Needles and Autonomy

The day after that conversation, I picked up the phone and called my former acupuncturist in San Diego. I told him I was going to leave the Navy and go to acupuncture school. I had already done a ton of research into various medical schools and modalities. The doctors I spoke with were disgruntled. They felt like they were drug pushers without autonomy or time to connect with their patients, and unable to be the healers they desired to be. A lot of the Physical Therapists I spoke with felt their hands were tied by insurance and mandatory protocols to gain reimbursement. But as an Acupuncturist, I could advise people towards wholeness and include nutrition, exercise, and meditation. I would also be able to order labs and MRI's for diagnosis. I could create my own palette for total health based on what individuals needed. This, to me, was the ultimate model of patient-centered care. And it felt exciting! Not to mention, having the ability to collaborate with whatever professionals I felt my clients would benefit from without needing permission or approval from outside sources. It absolutely felt like the scope with the most autonomy, which I craved.

I was surprised when he tried to strongly discourage me from going down this path. He told me how challenging it was to run your own business. Financially and energetically, it could be draining because you would only be able to make money when you were working. He sounded like he had seen some struggles in his practice and he didn't want to sugar coat any of it for me, which I appreciated. It was clear that it wasn't an easy profession. But I wasn't looking for *easy*. I was looking for *fulfillment*. And through the practice of awareness, I was learning to listen to my heart above the opinions of others.

It took two more years of me working through my doubts before pulling the trigger. I still identified as an athlete and was pushing myself, physically. Back in California, I had started to do 24 and 48 hour adventure races with some friends. We often finished top three in our races and had a lot of fun suffering together. Shortly after arriving in Pennsylvania, I got a call from the guys I raced with to compete in the Armed Forces Eco challenge in Alaska. This was a dream. It would be 4-5 days of non-stop racing and pushing myself to the limit. It was an opportunity to see if I had any quit in me. I decided to go for it and in standard Heidi fashion, I pushed myself ruthlessly to train for that event. I would mountain bike for hours, paddle for hours, and then run 10 miles and think nothing of it.

The race in Alaska was beyond grueling. We covered over 250 miles in the Alaskan outback with less than 6-8 hours of sleep, total. There was mountain biking, paddling, hiking, and rock climbing. I never knew I was capable of falling asleep while I was walking but it turns out, just like puking while swimming, it's totally possible. I experienced mild hypothermia when we got stuck in a fog bank and had to wait it out so that we didn't lose our bearings. On day two of racing, I was running down a rocky dried out river bed and twisted my knee terribly. It swelled up immediately and was super painful, just as it had been when I fell on the obstacle course. I didn't want to hold my team back so we duck taped it and I took a cocktail of Motrin and Tylenol every 6 hours and powered on. I was exhausted and in excruciating pain, but I was committed to finishing. I refused to be the reason our team had to pull out of the race. By the end of the race, I had lost all of my toe nails, and my hands and feet looked like I weighed 300 pounds. Talk about serious inflammation and body abuse.

I got my knee evaluated when I returned from the race. My meniscus was badly torn and my ACL was completely gone. The doctor talked me into surgery to prevent further degeneration in my knee, and he also recommended ACL replacement and suturing to fix my meniscus. I wanted to keep moving and the thought of having more damage if I didn't fix my knee now wasn't good.

Paul received new orders and would be moving up to Maine where the ship was being commissioned. Meanwhile, I was going in for surgery at Walter Reed Military hospital in D.C. Luckily, my wonderful sponsor parents from the Naval Academy offered their extra home for me to recover in Annapolis, Maryland. Paul stayed with me for a few days after the surgery, but then he had to get up to Maine. He was so amazing at helping me get through the recovery. During the process of nursing me back to health, he proposed a second time. I said yes, and this time, we decided to get married within the next few months. I felt like it was the right thing to do given he had been there for me through so much and no matter what my curious and adventurous heart sought to dive into, he was always there. I still didn't feel that deep connection or security, but I figured this was good enough. He was a good man, and we were great friends. Best friends!

Reluctantly Ever After

Paul and I went down to St Lucia, just the two of us, and got married. I remember waking up on the morning of our wedding *knowing* that I still had a deeper connection with someone else that wasn't available, and feeling confused by my decision to still go through with the wedding anyway. I thought, 'well, if this doesn't work out I can always get a divorce.' It feels terrible to admit to myself, and to you reading this now. Truthfully, there is still an inkling of shame attached. All of my siblings had gone through divorces and I desperately desired to be more successful in that area, especially after what my parents had gone through. But here I was, already giving myself an out. We had gone back and forth so many times over the years, I felt like I needed to give it (us) a real shot. Maybe if I committed (and got married), it would change things. Maybe my feelings would grow, romantically. I still thought I was the broken one for not feeling the way I wanted to in the relationship. I was also carrying the guilt of the hurt I had caused him over the years and I felt like I owed it to him to give it a try.

This feels like an important point to pause and reflect.

"I felt like I owed it to him." It falls in line with the statement of, 'I should' Have you ever heard about *shoulding* all over yourself? When the shoulds, coulds and woulds come into the picture, especially around major life decisions, do yourself a favor and **stop immediately** and **regroup**. If it's not a *hell yes*, it's a *hell no*. Period. What is in your highest and best is not selfish, it is a way of honoring yourself and everyone else in the process of being brave with your truth. Replace any notions of selfishness here with self honoring and let that be okay. You are worth the happiness you desire. Remember that.

Okay, moving right along.

The day after our wedding, we were on the beach with a few other couples we had met at the resort. I was laying on the beach with two of the women and they commented on how attractive my husband was. "Wow, can you imagine waking up next to that every morning?" exclaimed one. While the other lady mentioned how fortunate I was to be married to "such a specimen." Both comments made me cringe a little, and didn't land well at all. I think it just amplified my beliefs around relationships, and how I feel they're really so much deeper than surface level attraction. I absolutely want to look my best and I can appreciate an amazing physique. However, I crave deep, soulful connection. If a person has a few extra pounds or isn't what our culture deems beautiful, it means nothing to me. Which is why I think I had such a visceral reaction to their seemingly innocent comments. Every time someone mentioned how fortunate I was because my husband was so attractive, my internal response was always the same, "so what?"

We left St. Lucia and Paul headed back to his ship in Maine. My time in Mechanicsburg was coming to an end as well. My next set of orders took me back to San Diego, California to be the Assistant Supply Officer on the BonHomme Richard. Paul's ship was being built in Maine and was supposed to eventually be stationed in San Diego, CA too which meant we'd be together soon enough. Unfortunately, shortly after reporting to Maine, Paul was told the ship was now going to be stationed in Hawaii. The Navy said that Hawaii and California counted as co-location, and it was the best they were able to do. Not ideal, as this made doing my best to 'make it work' that much more challenging.

I came to San Diego pretty out of sorts. Looking back, I should have been impressed with myself! I had a job that was above my pay grade; the detailing officer had told me they pulled all sorts of strings to allow me to fill the job as a Lieutenant when it was actually a Lieutenant Commander's position. Which is hilarious, by the way, because in the Navy you get paid for your rank, not your job. The better performer you are, the more responsibility you get, but your pay remains the same. It's why so much talent ends up leaving the service. Because I was still super committed to my yoga and meditation practice, I was waking at 3:30am to do my asana practice and meditate so that I could be on the ship by 5:30am for Officer's call. I was still working hard to cultivate a sense of inner listening to find a deeper connection with myself. The more I did this, the more I realized the Navy was no longer the right fit for me. I was also pretty sure my marriage wasn't either.

New Adventure Awaits

I dropped my letter of resignation from the Navy and applied to acupuncture school. I was counseled by all of my Senior Officer's about what a foolish choice this was. My family was also very concerned about my departure from such a prestigious career. During my exit interview, my Executive Officer inquired, "Isn't an acupuncturist just a glorified prostitute of sorts?" I have no idea what kind of services he'd received, but I managed to keep my jaw from slamming onto the ground and just responded with a polite, "I think you may have the career confused with something different. You can actually receive a Doctorate and work in hospitals." I felt pressured to make it sound credible and worthy. All the while my soul was screaming for me to get the hell out of there!

It was an exhilarating and terrifying feeling to end my 9 year career in the Navy. I had been a part of the military institution for 14 formative years, if you count my time at the Naval Academy. I was taking a leap from structure and security into the unknown. I was free. And I was scared… *really scared*. I had so many conversations with my husband about how I was so uncomfortable depending on him and he reassured me it was all going to be fine. But it didn't feel fine. My heart didn't feel safe, and I was finally leaning into those little soul nudges with more discernment, questioning what they meant and what to do about them.

His ship was coming from Hawaii to be home ported in San Diego, and he wanted us to buy a house. Against my better judgement, I found a place and put my life savings into the down payment. I thought that maybe this was exactly what we needed to be 'all in.' Clearly he was committed; he married me and wanted to buy a house, after all. Nothing fixes a relationship like a joint financial commitment. (Insert: sarcasm.)

Soul Sisters

Acupuncture school began, and I could not have been happier for a fresh start down a new career path... something that actually felt exciting! On the first day, I met the most incredible woman. Her name was Claire and from the moment we met, I knew we had something special. I was drawn to her like a moth to a flame. She was vivacious and bright, and her smile lit up the entire room like sunshine. We hit it off instantly. It was another connection that felt like remembering or coming home. Little did I know at the time all the beauty that would transpire due to our chance meeting.

School allowed me the space and permission to get more in touch with my feelings. I had a class where we had to keep a journal about our daily feelings, which was super tough at first. At the time, the best I could manage were things like, *I feel hungry* or *I feel contemplative.* My entries were not used as the class example. But as I leaned into the discomfort, I could feel my intuition getting stronger. The yoga, meditation and journaling was paying off and I began to hear my heart more clearly.

During my process of awakening, I had a gut-wrenching feeling that Paul had been involved with a woman on his ship. When I brought it up, he made me feel super insecure and crazy for thinking this. So instead of pressing further, I ignored my intuition. And then I had a dream and in my dream, I saw the whole thing play out. I wanted to vomit. When I went to call him to talk about it, his line was busy. I was sure he was talking to her right then, which made me feel like I was going bananas. Crazy enough to check our phone records, in fact, and I was right. When I confronted him about it, he finally admitted to it all. I was beside myself as all of my insecurities came crashing down, right in front of my eyes. I was out of the military, and had just sunk all of my assets into a condo - *our* condo. I felt abandoned and betrayed. Initially, I kicked him out of the condo and convinced myself that we were done. However, he was deeply apologetic and begged me to continue working on our relationship together. I told myself that I didn't know what to do (note, I was still *working on* trusting my intuition at the time).

Claire was amazingly supportive through the entire process. She let me sleep on her couch and assured me that she would always be my soft place to land. We became so close in such a short period of time, something I am beyond grateful for to this day. I was pretty sure that my marriage was ending, but I knew that I had Claire and going forward, we had a plan to create a lot of healing for people together through acupuncture.

Paul and I went to counseling and decided we were going to try to figure things out. We agreed that even if we didn't stay together, we could at least move forward as better people, individually. We lived a very roommate-like existence for the next few years while I finished school. We even got a dog, using parenting to try and fix our relationship (never a good idea). We actually did an excellent job of training and raising her. She became my guardian angel and a really bright spot in our relationship. We also did a great job of staying distracted though, and simply co-existing instead of embracing a thriving partnership that brought us both fulfillment and joy.

'Til Death Do Us Part

In the last year of the Acupuncture program, Claire and I were studying together as we always did. We had a few glasses of wine and were talking about our lives when out of the blue she mentioned that she thought I would be such a great fit with her husband. I almost spewed out my wine. "What are you talking about?" I gasped. To which she very calmly stated, "well, you just get him. He's in the military and I'm all he knows. I just think it would be good for him to have another experience and you would be perfect together." I was so confused because they had such a great relationship. They adored one another! But it was just an example of her unconditional love. She just wanted me to be happy and she knew I deserved that. I didn't even want to be with my husband at that point, but there was no way I was secure or confident enough to be willing to imagine him with another woman. But that was Claire. Kind, compassionate, loving Claire. I was speechless. Over and over again, I was in awe of this woman.

Shortly after our conversation I started having frequent dreams that I was going to die. It got bad enough that I told my husband he should prepare something because I was having an awful, all-too-real premonition. He asked me to stop talking about it because it was really troubling. This whole 'intuition' thing was getting a little scary.

It was only 3 months after the dreams started that Claire found out she had stage four non-small cell lung cancer that had metastasized to her brain. I don't have words to describe what I felt when I got that news. Utter devastation and feelings of decimation don't cut it. Having my heart ripped out of my chest and smashed into 1,000 pieces on the floor? Maybe a little bit closer. Disbelief that this was the reality was accurate for sure. Bottom line: I was in absolute shock.

After processing what all of this meant, I pulled myself together and rallied. She was going to beat this, whatever it took. We even talked about how she would appear on Oprah telling her powerful tale of 'the healer that beat lung and brain cancer.' It was going to be epic. I spent every day with her after her diagnosis. I stopped going to most of my classes except for those I had to attend to graduate in a few months. I dedicated whatever time I could to being by her side, just as she'd been for me so many times before. Her husband was amazing at sharing her and receiving the support I so desperately wanted to give.

I went with Claire to her last radiation treatment for the brain tumors. I laid in her bed with her after the session and started crying. I told her I loved her so much and was so grateful for every moment we had shared. I felt so lucky that we had made so much out of our time together and felt so completely present with one another. She was a soulmate, this I knew. We both did. She hugged me and told me she felt the same way and it was all going to be okay. She thanked me for being there with her that day. The next step was for her to start chemotherapy.

But that night, I could not settle my spirit. I kept thinking I should go back, I should be with her. I didn't feel right at all. She only lived a quarter of a mile from my house, but it was late so instead, I went to bed. And then at 4am, I got a call from her mom who was in town and staying at Claire's. Through the phone she yelled, "Come quickly. Claire isn't breathing." And so I did. I arrived in a daze, as I ran up the stairs behind the paramedics and I clung to Claire's mom as they tried to resuscitate her. But it was too late. She was gone.

I struggled to get out of bed after she passed. How could someone so good leave this earth so soon? There are plenty of people that want to harm others and are caught up so miserably in their own pain, yet they get to live to ripe old ages. Why does someone so intrinsically pure depart before the world gets to fully benefit from their presence? It was so unfair. I felt robbed of precious time with her for myself, her family, and her husband. Why did I get to stay? Why was I still here? I started journaling, writing to her every day, asking for guidance through this profound sadness.

Grief is an interesting experience. It mutates, hides, and shows up in the most unexpected places. I thought going back to school would feel impossible and I mentally prepared myself to walk in and start bawling. Turns out, I was totally okay there. My self-protection kicked in, which allowed me to find some semblance of normalcy in the pain. And then, about a week later I walked into Discount Shoe Warehouse, a place that Claire and I had frequented together and of all places, that's where the water works began. I walked out of the store shocked and confused. I couldn't stop crying. I knew it was 'just a shoe store' but for us, it was a place where we had made so many special memories and moments that felt uniquely ours in how we connected. I couldn't go anywhere that was 'ours,' including the coffee shop or the store. And when our special song came on the radio, I would lose it, no matter who was in the car with me. I ached for her presence and felt so alone without her.

There was also a very palpable sense that none of the petty shit that we give meaning to really matters. The seduction of achievement and addiction to working to get ahead collapsed like a house of cards on itself. It was my own personal experience of the Ebineezer Scrooge dream with the ghosts of Christmas past. I was being visited by all of my beliefs and actions and evaluating their value against the stark reality of precious limited time. I really needed to get clear on who and what I was giving my energy to because it became blatantly obvious that our time is limited, and undetermined.

Nothing is guaranteed. Life is not fair. Control is an illusion. That meant I had to learn to listen to my heart and follow my inner guidance if I wanted to live a life of fulfillment, which I did. If I spent another minute doing anything I was 'supposed to' or 'should do,' I'd be wasting precious time. Time that I would never get back. I owed it to my soul to pay attention and act accordingly. I owed it to Claire, who didn't get the luxury of wasting any more time. I also became acutely aware of the importance of being in the now like never before. Most of the shit I worried about didn't matter one bit. It was up to me to create my reality in every single moment. I had the opportunity to live a lifetime in a single moment if I remained present and focused on what mattered most to me. So that was the commitment I made to myself, and to her, my sweet Claire, now an angel above.

My dreams of dying ended the night she died, and never came back again.

Claire is still a large part of our lives. My oldest daughter has Claire's middle name, Marie, as her middle name. We have a picture of Claire in their bedroom and talk to the girls about what a beautiful guardian angel they will always have looking over them. We are also extremely fortunate to have a great relationship with Claire's parents. They are part of our family and another set of grandparents to our daughters and that is how they relate to them. It is evident where Claire's compassionate and sweet nature came from. Her parents are incredible and have had to overcome so much through their loss, and still have such a positive outlook on life.

My oldest daughter had some dreams for a while where she told me that Aunt Claire was outside of her bedroom window waiting for a bus. I said, "Wow, isn't that sweet that she wants to check in on us before she goes somewhere?" She agreed, and hasn't mentioned much more about it lately. I don't know how much of that was a result of me talking about her as a guardian angel or how much of it is my daughter's powerful intuition. Either way, I don't want to scare her or overwhelm her, so I just let her share when she wants and encourage her curiosity. I know Claire is always with me. She gave me some of the greatest joys in my life. She was a sister, a teacher, a guide, and my dearest soulmate. I am a better person because of her. She softened me and showed me what unconditional love felt like. She changed the entire trajectory of my life. She affected so many, so powerfully in such a short time on this planet. Everyone that knew her is better for it, and I don't mean that in a cliché way. It's the absolute truth, and the ripple effect of her impact is still expanding today.

The loss of someone who means so much can never be filled. The best I can do is commune with her in my meditations and sometimes, much less often now, she visits me in my dreams. I have a special spot at the ocean where we used to go before she got sick. I often go sit there if I need to feel her. Dolphins always appear in some form when I really need her support. It's for sure her sign that she's still with me.

Another favorite way to connect with the people I have lost is through books. I have a few books, some angel cards and notes from Claire. I'll sit quietly and think about her and ask her for some guidance, then I'll open up a book of hers or pull an angel card from one of her old decks. It's incredible the insight that I receive. It's always exactly what I need to hear; the perfect words on the page or just the right card of encouragement. I know she has my back and while we can't share a glass of wine together, I still talk to her and she still talks back.

Lifeboat Lessons

1. Connect with your feelings and start journaling what the inner voice inside you is sharing. What are you feeling or avoiding feeling? Even if you don't really know, just start free-writing with whatever is taking up your mental space. Writing down the thoughts and ideas in your head is another great way to purge the monkey mind and create space for peace to manifest.

2. If you're experiencing heavy thoughts that have been weighing you down, those that don't serve much of a purpose anymore, you may even decide to gather the papers you've dumped your emotions onto and burn them after writing to fully release the overthinking patterns. Even just a few moments of journaling regularly can be extremely cathartic.

Note: You are welcome to have more structure around journaling where you note something you are grateful for, something that went well today, and/or something you would like to improve upon. I also find that giving yourself the space to just dump your thoughts on paper without structure can be very helpful and insightful, too.

CHAPTER 6

My Traveling Heart

"The real voyage of discovery consists not in seeing new landscapes, but in having new eyes." – Marcel Proust

Adventure feeds my soul. It offers me a new perspective and clarity as to what really matters in life. When I saw the beautiful children while traveling through Nepal, and all the families living simple lives while feeling so utterly fulfilled with the company of one another and content with their very modest means, I was forced to contemplate my own contentment. Travel invites me to challenge the questions of 'enoughness' within myself and what I have, in all capacities. Traveling is one of my first loves, and has simultaneously been one of my greatest teachers.

Claire's death birthed an intense need within me to get away and shake off my constraints, giving myself permission to reconnect with my heart and soul. Claire and I had planned a trip to study in China together before she got sick. Then, when she was diagnosed, I cancelled my trip, telling her that I had an ominous feeling that something bad was going to happen if I followed through with that trip by myself. I was right, too. If I'd gone, she would have passed while I was away and I never would have forgiven myself. Subsequently, I postponed my trip for the following year after graduating Acupuncture school, just a few months after Claire passed away. I then had to study for my license exam, which took place shortly after. I was in a bit of limbo between getting licensed and my trip to China when I found out that there was to be a yoga festival in India that my yoga teacher was going to be teaching at. It would be at the end of February, which meant that I had some time available to venture over to Nepal for a month before starting school in China. It all seemed to be magically falling into place.

Healer Heal Thyself

Things got even more synchronistic when looking back at another angel of a human in my life, whom I'd met at my first yoga class back in 1998. She struck me very similarly to Claire and no surprises here, we hit it off immediately. While we ebbed in and out of each other's lives over the years, we always remained in contact with one another. An instant point of connection was that we both had birthdays in November. Scorpio sisters, no doubt. We were deep thinkers and soul seekers. And we also shared a deep love of the water, both being swimmers and drawn to the sea by way of our watery nature. Every time we saw each other, it was as if only a moment had passed and we were back in sync, passionately sharing the magic that was unfolding in our lives. She had a beautiful way of seeing me and understanding me moment to moment; the same was true for me about her. We had a unique way of supporting each other in our conversations. Often we would realize we were actually giving advice to ourselves instead of the other and hearing ourselves out loud was the perfect container to make sense of it all. My intuition and trust in myself flourished around her; she was the most gorgeous mirror. Her name was Mariel. She was the salve needed to help heal the hole that Claire's physical absence had left in my heart.

Mariel was 13 years older than me and had grown children so while at different life stages, we both had active lives that pulled us in various directions. Mariel reached out to me when she heard of Claire's passing, which is when I mentioned the International Yoga Festival in India and her face lit up brightly. "We must go," she said. "Are you serious?" I asked. I really felt a calling to go, but I knew I wanted to share it with Mariel and I wasn't sure I had the courage to go without her. But she was in as she enthusiastically exclaimed, "this is perfect!" God, I loved her so much.

During this phase of my life, I was teaching yoga as a side hustle while going through Acupuncture school. It was my meditative safe place. I loved the way a nice flow connected with the breath aligned my body, mind and spirit. It reminded me of swimming. The studio where I was teaching advertised a Thangka exhibit. A Thangka is typically a Tibetan or Nepalese buddhist painting rendered on cotton or silk material. It's a spiritual tapestry used for representation of a teaching depicting a deity or buddhist story. I really connected with the philosophy of Buddhism and Taoism. I loved the self ownership and mindfulness that they supported and I felt the truth in it.

So I decided to go, and at the exhibit I met a lovely man that had brought some tapestries over from Nepal. He supported an orphanage with some of the money from the sales, which I loved. We got to talking and I mentioned that I was planning a trip to Nepal and wanted to do some hiking. He generously offered to put me in touch with a local family that would host me and arrange a trek as well. I couldn't believe how everything seemed to be lining up so perfectly. It was so synchronistic that the head of the Nepalese family, Dawa, was going to be staying in San Diego just 10 miles away from my home in a few weeks to visit. It was his first trip to the United States to visit his daughter who was attending school here. How was that even possible? I was invited to meet up with him and his family, and plan the trek and trip of a lifetime. I had created an intention for healing, and as I continued feeling into my heart, the universe was conspiring in my favor. I was in the flow.

Paul was in an MBA program at the time and didn't think it was worth the cost to come all that way to join me on my trip for a week or so. That was the most time he could take off. He did feel it was important for me to go do this trip and heal. Claire's husband, Brandon, was struggling, too. We were spending a lot of time together, wading our way through grief. When I discussed the plans of my trip with both of them, Brandon offered to join me for the month in Nepal. He thought we could go up close to Everest and leave some of Claire's belongings there. I thought that sounded great and Paul encouraged it. Brandon and I had both discussed how we wanted a tattoo to commemorate Claire's memory. I got mine shortly after she passed. I chose the sanskrit representation of 'bliss' or 'ananda' on the inside of my right wrist. Ananda is extreme happiness, one of the highest states of being and the energy that Claire and I shared. Brandon decided to include ananda inside his arm as well. His full tattoo has the mountain, Ama Dablam covering his shoulder, then a trail of Chinese characters representing the proverb, 'the journey of 1,000 miles begins with a single step.' Scattered along it are cherry blossoms to represent life and death. It's an exquisite tribute. Ama Dablam means 'Mother's Necklace,' and is named that because the long ridges on each side of the peak look like the arms of a mother protecting her child. No doubt, Nepal was calling.

Everything was set and I was off for my own Pray, Adventure, Learn experience. Two weeks in India with Mariel, four weeks in Nepal with Brandon, and four weeks in China to get to the root of my new occupation; it all sounded incredible and felt like the right and best thing to do for my heart. I remember walking through the San Diego airport feeling a little scared, being so detached and vulnerable. I chose to leave my cell phone behind because international plans weren't that reasonable at the time and instead, I decided I would rely on pay phones while away. I was consciously removing any possible distractions, committed to using this time to reconnect to myself and what might be next.

I had a layover in Chicago so I sat on the floor to do some yoga poses and meditation. An older man approached me and asked if he could sit with me in meditation. "Of course," I replied. He shared with me that his son had just been in a life-threatening accident. He had been hit by a car while riding his bicycle. He was on his way to see him and was praying he would make it before it was too late. My heart ached for him. I held his hand and we sat there in silence, both praying for each other. My yoga teacher witnessed the conversation and later shared with me that she felt I had a gift for walking people through grief. It was at that moment that I recognized one of my hidden strengths. I was also aware that I needed to give myself space to process and digest my own grief in order to have more room to give. 'Healer heal thyself' was taking on a different, and very real meaning for me.

Ananda to India

I had arrived, and met up with Mariel immediately. That gorgeous ray of sunshine; it was so comforting to have her by my side. Arriving in Delhi, India was an assault to the senses. All of them at once. First, there was the intense crowding everywhere, the smells of so many people and the pollution in the sky. Piles of trash so big they were like their own little cities. Amongst the trash were people and animals making a home. There were even families living in the medians of the freeways where a 5 year old was walking with her 1 year old sibling tucked under her arm. It was overwhelming in every way. I stood there in awe, taking it all in. I couldn't have dreamt of this kind of contrast between wealth and poverty. Yet in the midst of it all, everyone went about their daily lives. The poverty and the lack crushed my soul, but there was a profound sense of contentment in many of the locals I encountered along my trip. It was like someone had just turned up the volume on everything.

The next day we went to Gandhi's home. I felt a deep sense of peace there. It was a very spiritual experience for me. Mariel and I sat on the lawn and meditated for a while feeling into the essence of Gandhi's purpose and impact. The way he walked with such clarity and conviction amongst so much chaos was truly awe-inspiring. It guided me back inward to sit in silence and practice being in the eye of the storm. I recognized that some level of chaos was always stirring around me. I also realized the discipline necessary to be present to my breath and the moment, to avoid being pulled into the reactivity of my emotions and the actions around me. This disciplined state was exactly the environment that swimming and yoga provided. The real practice became taking that same level of awareness out of the pool and off the mat, and bringing it into each experience and interaction.

I had a beautiful opportunity to explore India. My intention was to witness all of India unfolding in front of me without judgement or attachment and instead, be in the practice of presence. I journaled at night about how being in India made me feel and I watched as my emotions ebbed and flowed through the journey. Quieting my mind and choosing to BE in each moment created such an expansive opportunity for growth, yes. But also, for healing. I was so grateful to be there, knowing it was exactly where I was meant to be at the time.

We moved on to the holy city of Rishikesh, where the Yoga Festival was being held. And we were fortunate to stay at Parmarth Niketan Ashram, the home of the festival itself. I had no expectations or agenda, which is my favorite way to travel - and I embraced it wholeheartedly. There was a packed schedule of classes available to attend, but Mariel and I felt compelled to attend the kundalini classes held every morning on the banks of the Ganges river. It was so wonderful to be outside next to such a powerful river practicing breathwork and movement with one of my favorite people. I was new to kundalini and the classes were very rigorous and challenging. Our leader, Gurmukh Kaur Khalsa was a bit of a yoga guru. She was a tough teacher, and had a unique way of motivating her students. Mariel and I thoroughly enjoyed it and felt invigorated and peaceful when the classes concluded.

On one particular day, we were surprised to find ourselves in a rebirthing ceremony, unsure of what to expect. We began with some rigorous asanas (yoga postures) and breathwork and then the class formed a tunnel by entwining hands overhead as each person passed through and everyone whispered, "welcome, we love you, I love you, you are cherished..." or anything along those lines that felt good for the person sharing. It was an incredible experience. Mariel and I both left that class with tear streaked cheeks and big smiles across our faces, completely awestruck with our experience. With each day, I felt like I was dropping more and more emotional baggage, and becoming clearer on what self-acceptance meant.

That same afternoon, after the rebirthing ceremony, we sat under a large tent and listened to Pujya Swamiji speak of peace and how to work toward attaining that within ourselves and the world. While he was speaking, a group of monkeys peaked through the folds of the tent above, throwing things down. One monkey even urinated on a woman several rows in front of me. The irony was not lost on me. It was the perfect metaphor for the monkey mind. Here we were, sitting in front of a Saint who was lecturing about peace while we all sat in our hot humid seats being assaulted by monkeys. Pujya Swamiji then shared about suffering and the human condition; how we suffer so much pain and feel that we need so many different managements to cope and exist: anger management, sex management, food management. But ultimately, we really only need one management: the management of our mind. I couldn't help but giggle. The monkeys surely were in on this gig and were definitely part of this magical teaching moment. I couldn't help but wonder how the lady that got peed on was doing with her mind management. It was easy for me to see the lesson and maintain my peace, but I wasn't the one that had been peed on.

Every evening we would gather on the steps of the Ganges for the Ganga Arati (lighting ceremony) at Parmarth Niketan. This ceremony is famous around the world. It includes chanting, singing, prayer and meditation. In the prayer, God's Grace by Pujya Swami Chitanand Saraswati he explains, "All day long the Divine bestows upon us the light of life, the light of grace and the light of His blessings. At arati we offer back the light of our thanks, the light of our gratitude and the light of our devotion." It was the most satisfying way to conclude the day. At the end of the first arati, I lit a candle for Claire, which I nestled in a paper boat with a flower and released down the Ganges with a prayer of gratitude, wishing her soul peace. Several in my group knew Claire and supported me in this beautiful ceremony. It was a sacred moment along the path to closure and my own inner peace.

After these sacred events, Mariel and I would go back to our room and have long deep talks. Those are the only talks fellow Scorpios know to have. We loved talking about the mystery of life and would shriek with delight when we discovered how paralleled our paths and desires were. Mariel was incredibly intuitive as well. We were both drawn to the esoteric and mysterious aspects of life, and loved a good challenge. She had a background in psychology and had studied acupuncture, energy work and a myriad of healing modalities. She was a beacon, a mirror, a teacher, a sister, a goddess. And just as I felt with Claire, my soul felt understood and at home whenever we were together. She would sit across the room on her bed, in the lotus position, and eagerly listen to my thoughts. With a glint in her eyes and whole body radiance, she would light up and say, "Oh Heidi that's so perfect... I love it! Don't you love how the universe works?" "Yes, it's amazing," I would say back to her. And I would feel exhilarated after every encounter. I wish everyone could experience a moment in her radiant presence. Much like Claire, Mariel had that kind of profound effect on everyone that knew her. I was incredibly fortunate to know two such women in one lifetime. What a tremendous gift.

We spent the final days in India in ceremony and ritual addressing any beliefs that were holding us back.

We were supposed to grab a coconut, give it the name of the belief and throw it in the river. My teacher suggested I name my coconut self-doubt. I threw that coconut with everything I had into that river. And while I'd wished that throwing this giant fruit would eradicate my deep-seated beliefs, it wasn't that simple. It was about having awareness and understanding that this belief was simply a game my mind liked to play with me when I got scared. The awareness allowed me to see the barrier and then my consciousness was able to push it aside. It was a tool to come back to any time I felt my self-doubt creeping in. I would imagine myself throwing the coconut back into the river as a way to release old thoughts, while turning up the volume on better feeling beliefs in their place.

By the end of the trip, pretty much everyone had gotten sick with Giardia, or some sort of stomach issue. I was the only one in our group that stayed healthy up to this point. I felt super lucky and took on the healer responsibility of keeping my friends hydrated and supported.

When it was time to say good-bye to my group, I did so in humble gratitude as I left my new friends and Mariel, and ventured on by myself to Kathmandu, Nepal where I met up with Brandon.

A Journey of a Thousand Steps

I was so excited to get off the plane in Nepal and see Brandon's heart-warming smile. I threw my arms around him and hugged him hard as he lifted me up. We were reunited and it felt so perfect. I felt like a different person than the one who'd left San Diego just a few weeks earlier. Dawa, our host, met us both at the airport and took us to his home where we would stay before we began our 21-day trek. It was a good thing we had 3 down days before we started hiking because I inevitably got hit with an awful case of Giardia and needed time to recover. Luckily, Brandon was traveling with antibiotics and came to my rescue so that I could mend and get back on my feet in time to trek without delay.

The first night at Dawa's house, I felt this irresistible urge to be with Brandon; he felt the same. We were like magnets being pulled toward one another. It felt like it was beyond our control, no matter how many excuses our brains gave us. There was an intense physical attraction that overrode any rational parts of our brain. My heart was bursting. It absolutely felt like this was meant to be.

While recovering from Giardia, Brandon looked over me and kept me company while I lay shivering in bed with a fever and terrorized guts. He climbed into bed and held me tight to warm me up. It was healing and I felt at home pressed up next to him. He reached his arm tightly around me and I kissed his hand. This was my person. My heart knew it, my body felt it, and my brain finally gave in. He helped me get my gear together for the start of our trek and was so encouraging about my physical state, ensuring me that I was going to be fine. His confidence helped mine soar.

We had an incredible trek planned. Dawa's brother, Pemba was going to lead us and his nephew, Bala would carry our main bag. Brandon and I each hiked with our own water and daily supplies, but Bala was our sherpa that hauled our sleeping bags and extra clothes. Bala was half my size and I would put his aerobic endurance up against the best athletes in the world.

We drove to a town called Jiri and from there we began our trek. The idea was to complete the hike that Sir Edmond Hilary hiked when he summited Everest in 1953. Jiri to Everest base camp required ascending 3,000 meters at over 170 km starting at 2,370 meters. The terrain is moderate to challenging, but it is just a walk. We would then walk back from Everest base camp to Lukla and fly out to Kathmandu. Many people fly directly into Lukla and trek to Everest and back, but I really wanted to hike the lower regions to be able to connect with the people and culture of the surrounding Everest area. And I'm so grateful that we did. We had the most extraordinary experiences along the way.

As the trek moved along, Brandon and I talked about our lives. I talked about my family growing up and he shared his own stories with me. We laughed a lot. The lodges we stayed in were mostly peoples' homes that they opened up to the trekkers to make a living. We shared a room and snuggled up with one another every night. We were a couple in that new stage of puppy love, but there was also an odd sense of familiarity. It felt natural and easy to be together. He would take my underwear and sports bra and wash it in the freezing water so that I didn't have to. He was looking after me as if we had an established rhythm of togetherness. We were blissed out with one another. At the same time, we were both struggling with having such clear and deep feelings for one another so soon after Claire's passing. And I had the additional layer of still being married, although unhappily.

About 2 weeks into our trek we arrived at a village called Tengboche. Tengboche is an important Buddhist Monastery with the largest Gompa (religious building or meditation room) in the region built in 1923. From here you can also see Ama Dablam if the weather is favorable. We were really looking forward to getting to see the impressive peak that Brandon had tattooed on his shoulder.

When we arrived, it was misting and extremely overcast. We were both disappointed given it didn't seem like we would get the opportunity to see what we'd traveled so far for. So instead of waiting around for the fog to lift, I recommended that we go to the Monastery to listen to the monks' chant. The most hypnotic and mesmerizing sound filled the monastery. I got chills the moment we entered, and found a place to sit and marinate in the juiciness of the collective energetic vibration. I have no idea how long I was sitting for, but it felt like an eternity in a moment. It was euphoric. Then out of nowhere, I felt a tap on my shoulder and as I looked up, no one was there. Across the room, I noticed Brandon was leaning against a wall with tears streaming down his face. I walked over and took his hand and we walked out of the building, about 400 yards to a clearing. The sun had come out and the clouds were lifting and as we looked back, there was Ama Dablam in all her glory, visible behind the monastery. I couldn't believe it. We were both overcome with emotion and simultaneously expressed our love for one another. I was overcome with love and clarity and I felt Claire in that place. So did Brandon. We both felt like we had her blessing to explore our connection further.

The rest of the trip was mostly blissful. We ascended Kala Patthar, which gave us a glorious view of Everest, Nuptse and Changtse. Kala Patthar is the highest altitude you can reach without a permit and is just under 19,000 feet. At that summit we left some of Claire's items and took a moment of silence to honor her memory. We loved her so much and were so grateful for this new love she led us to. We both still struggled with moments of guilt. It was hard to reconcile the grief of loss with the profound joy we felt for one another. We also wondered what people were going to say or think when we came home. Our conclusion was that it didn't matter, which seemed like an easy enough conclusion to stomach when you are sheltered from the real world.

Coming down off the mountain was tough. I was heading to China by myself. Brandon was going back to San Diego, and I was deeply in love. It was kind of perfect that I had planned a month-long solo adventure in China to be alone with my feelings.

Integrating Feelings + Integrative Medicine

I had a few friends from Acupuncture school that were absolute lifesavers. I was able to confide in my roommate and one of my best male friends was also on the trip. What was I going to do? I had to end my marriage. I had to put a period at the end of one sentence before I started the next (I happen to have an affinity for run on sentences). Let's just say closure, as we know from my past, hasn't been a strength. I equated closure to failure, and I was also afraid of the pain I would cause.

China was an interesting overall experience for me. It was the first time I felt really different. When I entered a clothing store, I had a lady tell me they didn't have XXL and she ushered me out of the door. I am not a large person, by the way, and it definitely didn't help my body image issues. It's a different way of interacting than what I was accustomed to. I also really struggled with some of the ideology. I was told I had to participate in an event that I didn't want to be involved in. The propaganda department of the hospital and University where we were learning had an agenda. They wanted us to participate in the video they were making to show that foreigners were providing aid to a recently decimated area from an earthquake. I was opposed to participating because I felt it was not an accurate depiction of what was happening. I caused a bit of a fuss and our chaperone from the United States was really glad I was heading home because I had worn out my welcome.

I had a really nice time with my classmates. We took a trip to Tibet, which was really amazing and a little troubling as well. I sensed the oppression of the Tibetan people. They did not feel safe to speak freely. It was still a beautifully spiritual culture and I was beyond grateful for the opportunity to visit Lhasa and touch the door handles and building of the lineage of Lama's that had come before us. It was a very special opportunity. It was very enlightening as well to see how seamlessly traditional Chinese medicine was woven into healthcare along with western medicine. I thoroughly enjoyed seeing herbology being used in

IV's in the medical wards. Surgery was a last resort after alternative modalities had been exhausted. I got to see how injection therapy for joints was used in conjunction with Acupuncture and moxibustion. It was really encouraging to see how truly integrative the medicine I was studying could be.

The time went by quickly and while I was in China, I was talking to both Paul and Brandon when I could. I decided not to tell Paul about what had happened between Brandon and I over the phone. Brandon saw Paul occasionally back in San Diego and had not addressed it with him either, as they were planning a homecoming party for me together. How awkward.

Rising Phoenix

It was evident to Paul, when I got back to San Diego, that things were strained between us. He had sensed it in our phone calls. He described me as distant, and I definitely was. The day after my homecoming party, where Paul could see the connection that Brandon and I had, he went through my bag from my trip and found my Journal. He read all of the thoughts and feelings I had discovered while I was away. I was over visiting Brandon at the time and Paul came over, bursting through the door in a rage and confronted both of us. What could we say? Paul told me he was devastated. He accused Brandon of stealing me from him. I felt terrible. Brandon felt terrible as well. He was struggling with feeling the way he did so soon and affected by how people would react so he pulled back.

Paul convinced me to do another round of counseling. It was short lived because he was headed off in a few months to Iraq for 6 months. I was diving deep inside to get in touch with what I really wanted. I knew what I felt in Nepal was so distinctly clear. I came home, back to myself over and over again through journaling, meditation and yoga. A few friends of mine reacted very strongly to the idea of Brandon and I. Most of them didn't know the full story of how Paul and I had struggled; they just saw this union that triggered them in uncomfortable ways and they didn't know how to process it. It was interesting to witness. A friend of mine had mentioned that community structure can be like a mobile (the ones you hang from the ceiling). When one of the members shifts their composition, it affects the whole mobile and it can make some feel great, and others extremely uncomfortable. I was definitely experiencing that. As I was changing and moving to a place of my desires, it had a ripple effect around me and sometimes, it created tsunami-like reactions in others.

I created a vision board of what I wanted. I was not going to go through all of this to just go back to old habits and belief systems. I made a specific chart of what I wanted in my relationship and what love looked like to me. I drew a big heart and put love in the center. I wanted a passionate, kind, strong, adventurous, charitable, selfless love. I wanted to feel safe. I wanted equality and freedom to be myself, completely.

Paul did me a huge favor. He went on deployment and fell in love with another woman. He denied it the whole time he was away. He even came back to me. I think he had the belief that he needed to see if he still had any love for me. I don't think he was able to just be honest with me and end it because he was controlling me on some level and probably okay with causing me hurt so that I could feel what he felt. Whatever it was, it made the whole thing so much more messy and painful than it needed to be. It took him a long time to let go and it took me just as long to leave.

There are relationships that are meant for a reason, a season and very rarely, a lifetime. We had clearly been meant for a season and we were in denial that summer had ended. I wish I had the courage to listen to my heart earlier and avoid the pain I caused Paul. That is my biggest regret. I also acknowledge that we were willing participants in each other's pain. I think we just had to do the dance to grow. It had to get extraordinarily messy and abundantly obvious that it wasn't meant to be for us. Maybe that sounds like a cop out, but having personally been through it, there didn't feel like there was another way.

I feel like the growth I experienced as a result of that relationship massively contributed to who I am today. I am truly grateful for all of it. He was and is a wonderful man. He got me through some really tough spaces and for all that we shared, I will be forever grateful. I had to get so uncomfortable that I would not and could not settle. All of what I thought I was supposed to do and be was disintegrating into a glorious mess. It was both painful and liberating at the same time. It was my phoenix moment.

Brandon and I finally gave ourselves permission to explore the love we discovered in Nepal. It was the most glorious YES I have ever experienced in my life. He fulfilled my vision board intention and brought even more to the table than I knew I wanted. Again, the universe was conspiring for me, I just had to step out of my own way and receive it.

I had felt a funny feeling ever since my romantic feelings for Brandon developed; a new desire to have children. I loved him so deeply and it felt so safe that I knew I wanted to raise little people with him. He had no intention or desire to have children prior to us connecting; he and Claire had no plans to have kids. She had even told me early on in our relationship that I was going to be the one to have kids and she would be the cool Aunt that spoiled them rotten. Man, she knew so much.

On an amazing trip to one of my most favorite places, Maui in Hawaii, Brandon asked me to marry him. I was beside myself. I loved it so much that I asked him to ask me again four or five times. It felt so perfect. Every part of me was screaming YES!!! My life was full of magic, and I felt more in the zone than ever.

Fertility Freak-Out

We had a magical engagement and decided to get married shortly after. We had explored a bunch of expensive options for a ceremony and then decided it was about us and got married at the courthouse witnessed by our friends and family that could attend. My dog, Koda, was our attendant. She was perfect. We took an incredible trip to Bhutan for our honeymoon. It just made sense that we would go back to the magical Himalayas to celebrate our love and commitment to one another.

While we were in Bhutan we visited the temple of fertility. I had to coax Brandon to roll the dice. Turns out, he rolled the most fertile number. Our guide was really impressed. The trip to Bhutan was so perfect. We had a full week of hiking in the high Himalayas just he and I, again with a guide and group to feed us. Everything felt right.

Shortly after coming back to San Diego, I had a dream. In the dream, a red headed girl that looked strikingly similar to Merida from the Disney movie, Brave appeared to me, hands on her hips. "Are you going to have kids or what?" she demanded. "Because if you aren't, I have to find other parents." It was powerful. I was 39 years old and I was wondering if we would even be able to have kids. I had never been pregnant in my previous marriage, not even by accident. What if it was too late? We decided we should try because it might take us a while.

Brandon came home from a work trip just for a few days and we removed the goalie one time. I didn't even think anything of it because I was nowhere near ovulation. We were separated for a bit afterwards due to his work requirements. Several weeks later, while working on some athletes at the CrossFit Games, I found myself unable to stop crying over the silliest things. I was super emotional. *What is going on?* I thought to myself. I even called Brandon and told him I needed to make an appointment with the doctor because I was not myself.

After the CrossFit competition, we took a short trip to Catalina. While we were there, a group of deer came right up to me. The momma came up to my hand and nuzzled me. It was the most surreal experience. "Well how about that," I said to Brandon. It was like she was trying to tell me something. "Maybe she is trying to tell you that you're pregnant," he said. "What? That's impossible," I responded.

A day later, I woke up in the early morning and took a pregnancy test. It was positive. I was thrilled and terrified at the same time. I got back into bed with Brandon and started crying. "You're pregnant," he said. "I am," I cried. My stomach churned and my breath shortened. I had a crushing feeling as to the reality that so little was in my control. I could eat perfectly, do everything right and yet, I would still have no control over how this little being fully developed inside of me. I couldn't ever ensure she would be perfectly safe. I was terrified.

The issue of control was front and center and little did I know, it was going to hit me again. My pregnancy was going great. At the 16 week point we decided to take a trip to Hawaii and celebrate this amazing being that was growing inside of me. At the resort, we were watching all of these families with kids having the best time and day dreaming of what our experience with our sweet bundle was going to be like. I went up to our room and I had a voicemail on my phone. When I listened to it, it was my nurse practitioner and she sounded very distressed. She said she was very sorry to leave such a message over voicemail, but my tests came back positive for Down syndrome and she wanted me to be more fully evaluated as soon as possible when I returned from our trip. I slid down the wall and sat dumbfounded on the cold tile floor of our hotel room. I couldn't breathe.

Brandon came over to me and I told him what I had heard and we sat together and he held me as I started crying. I was in utter disbelief. This wasn't part of what I had imagined in our future. I called several friends to get advice. One of my dearest friends has a child with Down syndrome. I called her and she was incredible in her ability to console me and simultaneously, give me an epic pep talk.

That night, we drove over to Kailua Beach, a true spiritual sanctuary for me. We sat at the base of a tree on the beach and decided we were okay. What we could control was ourselves and how we handled this going forward. We were going to put our love and trust in one another and just take it one step at a time. We were having this baby and going to raise it in the most loving and supportive way, no matter what. We had a few more days on the island to make peace with the news and our decision. I was so grateful to be walking this path with Brandon. I knew that no matter what, we were okay.

When we got home, it turned out that the news wasn't accurate. Those early tests my nurse practitioner was referring to just put me in a high percentage of having a baby with Down syndrome. It was not definitive. We met with a genetic counselor, proceeded with further blood testing and had a high level ultrasound. Turns out that our baby girl was just fine. At 16 weeks, she was already giving me a run for my money and teaching me to let go and trust.

Biggest Blessings

This little girl had plenty of wisdom to share and a bit of sass with how she went about it. I felt like I was already getting to know her. I told Brandon that we needed to choose a name that was elegant but edgy, so we settled on Isabel, or Izzy for short.

Parenting is the most awesome adventure I have been on so far. I can't believe I thought it wasn't for me. That's the cool thing about life though. Things are exactly as they should be when they happen, we just have to surrender and trust in the perfect unfolding. My life has certainly shown me that. The more I try to force it, the more messed up it becomes. Isabel was already teaching me the lesson of surrender and trust - and she wasn't even born yet!

There is no doubt that Izzy chose me; that dream was foreshadowing. There have been times where I've found myself trying to force her to be the way I wanted her to be to establish control. And in the end, we were both left angry and frustrated. I hated that she wanted to be right so much, but then I was just mirroring that back to her. Then I got perspective. I heard the greatest story and I think about it when I start to go into control-mode.

There was a man that owned a labrador. Every day, he would force the lab to take fish oil because he knew it was good for him and the lab would fight back. One day, the lab knocked the bottle from the man's hands and it broke onto the kitchen floor. The angry man was about to yell at the dog when the dog started licking the oil off the floor.

This story resonates big time for me when it comes to my dynamic with Izzy. She needs to do it her way. It is also a lot of what I experienced as a child. She is my feisty, red-headed mirror.

When I get triggered with her behavior, I do my best to hold space for her. I breathe and I meet her where she's at, and soothe her down from her heightened emotions. I give her space to calm down. When we are both in a good space, we talk about what we experienced and how we can manage it better next time. I am not afraid to apologize to her when I overreact or behave in an inappropriate way. For I, too, am human. She knows that I love her absolutely, unconditionally. I do still hold her accountable for her actions and she has consequences if she behaves inappropriately, but she understands the consequences and we discuss it. I tell her that she can tell me anything she wants, even if it's something she doesn't agree with, but she must do so in a kind and respectful manner. I'll discuss it with her and I'll hear her out. That doesn't mean I will change the consequence, but it creates an opportunity for discussion and for her to be heard and appreciated. It's not perfect, and we don't always get it right, but the love and intention is there.

I don't know if it would change who I am if I had been handled in this manner. I don't know how it will impact Izzy. I do know that it feels kind. It feels vulnerable and authentic. And she is an incredible human.

The experience of having children has allowed me to see myself more clearly. It has unearthed baggage that I have been holding onto and given me the opportunity to unpack it. I am aware that my kids teach me more than I teach them sometimes, and I am grateful for it. I also know that they learn more from my example than my extensive pontifications. Izzy told Brandon, in a very sweet way, that sometimes when he takes a really long time to explain things she did wrong, it's really annoying and frustrating. I feel her pain and I appreciate her honesty. We both have the opportunity to cultivate more patience.

Izzy is my little rule follower, achiever, and perfectionist. She wears her heart on her sleeve and overthinks everything. She's the perfect mixture of Brandon's and my strengths and weaknesses. She is the most incredibly thoughtful and caring little person I have encountered. She chastised me once when I described her friend at school as having some special needs. She said, "Mom, she is just shy." She got the whole class to support and rally around this little girl in a wheelchair. So much so that her teacher asked me what I did to create such a compassionate leader. "I didn't," I said. That's just Izzy.

Brandon and I were fortunate to be able to bring another sweet soul into the world shortly before my 42nd birthday. Gabrielle, or Gabby, is our monkey. She brings levity to Izzy's deep thoughts. She is extremely athletic and is less affected by people's opinions. Because of this trait, it can be hard to discipline her. We have struggled at times to find anything that makes her want to change her behavior. Gabby wants to be just like her sister, but recognizes that their personalities are very different. When Izzy gets hyper-emotional, Gabby sits back perplexed and often shrugs her shoulders and walks away. She may even throw in an eye roll and say, "Izzy's freaking out again, Mom." She says exactly what's on her mind without concern of how it's received.

On her second birthday, the dog ate half of Gabby's Elmo cake. It was a seven layer cake of Elmo's face that ended up looking like Elmo had been cast on, <u>The Walking Dead</u>. Gabby's response was, "it happens." She is more likely to roll with stressful situations. Her matter of factness often cracks us up and provides for great stories. Just recently, when Claire's parents were visiting us she asked Claire's mom why she makes Claire's dad do everything. We all died and Claire's dad smirked with appreciation that someone recognized his efforts. She is also the perfect combination of our strengths and weaknesses.

Parenting has provided plenty of challenges to our relationship. We are on the same page most of the time and do make our relationship a priority. That is critical. But it can't be all about the kids, all the time. If you forget to water your garden with love and appreciation for each other, the garden won't survive. Date nights and one on one get-aways to nurture our ongoing romance are essential. I feel like we have done a pretty good job of making our connection a priority. There were harder times after the girls were born where there was so little sleep that it felt a bit like survival mode. The important part there was that we had a deeply nurtured love for one another and great communication so we were able to talk about the challenges we were facing. Brandon felt like he wasn't a priority for a while and maybe even slightly neglected. We were able to talk about it and find ways to connect, even if it was over a foot rub and snuggling before succumbing to the exhaustion from the day. I am so grateful that he sees our partnership as a journey. Sometimes, the weather is spectacular and the road is easy and fruitful. Other times, one of us is breaking trail 5 feet ahead and the other is just doing their best to hang on through the storm. The beauty is that we are both willing to break trail and recognize that neither one is superhuman alone but together, we make a pretty spectacular team.

Parenting is a balancing act, or maybe more like filling your plate at a buffet. There is so much to choose from, but choosing what's most nourishing will ultimately support what serves you and your family best, without over-filling or under-filling your plate. It changes constantly and flexibility is critical to surviving and thriving. Traveling *was* my greatest teacher...

Now, my guru is parenthood.

Lifeboat Lessons

1. One of my favorite centering exercises is to remember that I am not my thoughts and that my emotions are transient. With that intention in mind, begin box breathing. Box breathing is picking a number that you can maintain for an inhale, and holding your breath in for that same count, then breathing out for that same count and holding your breath on the exhale for the same count. Example: Breathe in for 4, hold for 4, breathe out for 4, hold for 4, and repeat.

2. Continue box breathing for 3-5 minutes. When you are done, simply sit for another 2-5 minutes and just notice any changes in your state. If your mind still has chatter, try another few minutes of breathing with inhaling "I" and exhaling "am." Yes, you are. Just as I am - here and now.

CHAPTER 7

Meant For Hard Things

"She was unstoppable, not because she did not have failures or doubts, but because she continued on despite them." – Beau Taplin

I don't back down from challenges. In fact, I often seek them out. As an overachiever, I am mildly addicted to the realization that I can do more than I think. I crave that endorphin release I feel when I push myself into a place that is scary and unknown, something I have held true since childhood. The reason I find it so seductive is because once the task is complete, there's a beautiful glimpse into the absolute expansiveness of the human spirit. If I can dream it, I can achieve it - this I know to be true. Some of my innate drive, dedication and discipline likely comes from my genetics. Writing this book has provided me with the opportunity to reflect back on the lives of my mother and father and the incredible amounts of adversity they overcame. Knowing what I know about their stories of resilience, it's no surprise that some of that was passed down to me, and my siblings. We are definitely a family of 'make shit happen' paired with a 'whatever it takes' attitude.

The way that I was nurtured certainly had a massive impact as well, and it's been a real gift to take the time to reflect on how I was raised. I can see where I have laid judgement and told myself stories that were true to me once upon a time. Giving myself the space to digest it all in its entirety and then to see how the ingredients were necessary for the end result, however, is something very different.

Throughout my life, it was always easy for me to criticize my mom's tactics. The extreme measures she took to ensure that I had excellent manners and behaved appropriately would be viewed by many outsiders as 'over-the-top.' She always had very high expectations of me and would not hesitate to make every correction she deemed necessary to ensure that I ended up with a stellar outcome. She was extremely disciplined and expected the same of her children. She could also be extremely critical. I see it now, even more so, when I FaceTime her with my kids and she comments on how unruly their hair is, or heaven forbid, the way my 2 year old eats blueberries with her hands. I realize that her critical eye comes with the best intentions. However, it was hard as a child not to feel the constant weight of what felt like judgement, as it fed the story that nothing I did was ever good enough for my mom. Which led me to further question my own enough-ness, period.

Unsolicited Advice

After my first daughter was born, my mom's critical nature felt amplified and really struck a nerve. It was one thing to criticize me, but to be critical of my babies brought out my inner momma bear. She was more than happy to offer unsolicited advice and disapproval on much of what I did. When I spoke to my dad about this he laughed and said, "That's your mom! Good luck ever doing it the right way." For the first time in my life, I felt real empathy for my dad. I could sense that he also felt like he was never enough for her, and I can imagine it wasn't easy for him, either.

My siblings and I have talked about this issue at length. We've all felt the effect of her judgment. They have also been criticised by my mom about how they are raising their children. We often commiserate about how we can't seem to do anything right or well enough for her; it's an ongoing theme. The interesting part is that all of us, my dad included, are equally in awe of her resilience and strength. She is a brilliant force.

When I was around 9 years old, I mowed the lawn for my mom. This was when we were living in a house, just the two of us, after she and my dad separated. I remember anticipating her approval and accolades when she came home, beaming with pride at the job I'd done. However, when she got home, she looked it over and commented on how my lines weren't straight enough followed by all the ways that I could have done it better. Her delivery and tone felt harsh and dismissive. In turn, I felt like a failure. In all fairness, the German language isn't gentle in it's delivery and I can't help but wonder if part of it was just the way she was used to offering information, albeit bluntly. It definitely had a militant feel to it. I was merely a child trying to win the approval of my mother, one of my hero's, yet it wasn't good enough. A story that I told myself which said: *if nothing I do is good enough, that means that I am not good enough either.*

More recently, I made a point to ask her why she was (and still is) so critical. Her response was, "why would you want to do something poorly or wrong when there is a right way to do it?" A very German response, void of any real emotion, and acutely reflective of how she was raised. That same critical eye and high standard that pushed me to excel and expect nothing but the best from myself was also one of the things that caused me to question myself, time and time again.

After sharing this story with a friend he stated, "That's why you're so good at so much of what you do, Heidi." He saw it all in a very positive way, which I appreciated. And while that is likely true, it didn't change how it made me feel in the moment. My enough-ness was reliant on my ability to earn her approval. Which meant, failing would only lead to further disapproval but also, disappointment. I told myself that I had to succeed in order to be loved. Part of my drive to push harder and prove people wrong was to show others that I was worthy and acceptable. In succeeding, I was also doing my best to prove this point to myself.

Which brings me to having a growth mindset. Learning more about what it means to have a fixed vs.

growth mindset, and then having the opportunity to see it firsthand as a parent while reflecting on how I was raised and the mindset of my parents… all I can say is WOW! I have found this concept to be an absolute game-changer for myself and my children and I've often wondered how things may have been different had I grown up in a growth mindset household.

Growth mindset allows for constant evolution as a human. Nothing is fixed, labels aren't given, and feedback is shared in a nurturing way. Failure is seen as a learning opportunity and is kept separate from a person's character. Please don't mistake this for coddling or lowering the bar. I won't be able to do the whole concept justice in this short piece. Suffice it to say, having a growth mindset unlocks human potential and eliminates the impulse to pigeonhole individuals and their capabilities. Instead of labeling a person as 'good' or 'bad,' 'smart' or 'stupid,' the actions are evaluated for their own merit. It takes away the shame that can come with not feeling smart, good, or worthy. Instead, it becomes an evaluation of the action, providing feedback as to how you can improve on it in the future. It's a really powerful practice to adopt, and one that I believe in wholeheartedly.

Having my own athletic experiences now and working with so many high achievers, I have also found it imperative to review what went well *first* and then, focus on what we want to improve upon with total ownership of the experience. A recap after every event is essential for growth, and I believe it can and *should* be an empowering experience. From a positive platform, there's a greater likelihood for openness and acceptance of effective criticism. If my mom had simply acknowledged my effort in the grass mowing situation *first*, and expressed her appreciation for my hard work, I would have been encouraged to mow the grass again. She could have come back later and given me some pointers and I would have been open and eager to learn and execute accordingly. Instead, I often tried to get out of tasks because I knew it was just going to bring about a heavy dose of not-good-enough-ness and annoyance on her part. She would eventually just decide to do it herself because I either took too long to do it or it wasn't up to her level of satisfaction. Please don't disregard ownership in this picture. I absolutely believe in taking complete ownership of our actions in every situation. There are no excuses or blame allowed in these evaluations, just the facts and an opportunity to process the emotions involved.

Patience, something I didn't grow up with a good example of, is a critical asset in becoming a successful parent, friend, and coach. Hell, of being a human, in general! We are not born pre-programmed to know the standards and rules of the world. And thus, we must create them.

Captain of the Soul

My Mom's response to my feedback on this whole situation was that I should just know that she loves me, and that she shouldn't have to constantly compliment me on my achievements to believe this. One of her critiques of me is that I need constant stroking and validation. I guess that's one way to look at it. However, I don't see it as such. The truth is, she has never told me that she thinks I am doing a good job as a parent, and she often comments as to how fortunate I am with how my life has turned out. She sees it as luck. I, however, don't agree with the assessment that I am 'lucky' or in need of validation. I do believe that 'words of affirmation' is one of my primary love languages. And I believe words of affirmation are essential to help any child build confidence in learning a new skill. Adults, too! Motivation becomes easier when you feel a sense of success based on your effort. Luck is created, not just happenstance. I worked really hard to create great opportunities for myself. The luck of being in the right place at the right time was simply the universe conspiring *for me* as a result of the decades of effort I put into the equation. Patience is paramount, no matter who you're leading. It is not a virtue that anyone in my family has in their DNA. I am highly aware of this and because of this awareness, I continue to choose to lean into that weakness to create strength as much as possible.

Everyone in my family did receive more than an ample amount of drive. Undoubtedly, we are an achieving group of disciplined individuals. I don't want to label, but I think most people will agree that the Germans of my mother's era were a very disciplined group of individuals that believed there was an absolute right way to do things. There is a measure of pride in this belief. Discipline is doing things even when you don't want to, understanding that achieving results requires effort. My mom survived the war this way. When my mom was a young girl, she had to run into a burning warehouse to try to save food for her family. Her life depended on it. The twist my mom taught me to add to the concept of discipline is that your attitude about how you go about it is also a choice. She took every opportunity to remind me of how I was the only one that could manage my emotions. Fair point.

One of my mom's favorite examples is a morning cup of coffee. You decide if you need that cup of coffee to put you in a good mood, or you can wake up deciding that you are in a good mood and simply enjoy the cup of coffee. The attitude you maintain while you are in a position of suffering makes all the difference. War taught my mom this, and she passed it on to me. It goes back to Swamiji's statement about management of mind. Only you can decide how you want to feel about things and what attitude you cultivate. An attitude of gratitude is a popular saying now because in that state of mind, everything feels easier.

There is an incredible man named Captain Charlie Plumb. He spoke to my class at the Naval Academy about his 7 years as a prisoner of war. He shared how he managed to maintain a positive outlook over those 7 years and come home with PTG - Post Traumatic Growth. He looked for the good in every moment and somehow, he found that speck of good he was searching for and managed to focus on that rather than the overwhelming bad that surrounded him. The seed he nurtured every day was gratitude. He learned how to be unconditionally grateful in even the most adverse situations. Not unlike Viktor Frankl from the book, Man's Search For Meaning where he finds the strength of his spirit in a concentration camp. These men, along with my mom, have recognized the secret sauce which is, that we alone manage our minds. When we cultivate that management with discipline, we become the captains of our soul.

The only way to do this is to practice with unrelenting discipline from several angles. Tony Robbins encourages people to cultivate a feeling and then solidify that feeling in the body by doing a physical move. It's a neurolinguistic practice. I have a tattoo on my wrist that reminds me to be grateful in moments where doing so might feel hard. I also meditate and journal on gratitude. I now do a journaling practice with my kids, too. We have so much to be grateful for but often in our pursuits for greatness, it's easy to get caught up in what's missing.

Meditation is a beautiful practice, and so critical as a way to check in with ourselves and what our soul needs. I often find that when cultivating gratitude, where patience becomes extremely difficult, it's my body's way of asking me to put on the brakes. Irritability, for me, is often my check engine light coming on and letting me know that my plate is overloaded and out of balance. The only way for me to get clarity on that is to meditate, journal and exercise. A really good night's sleep can often do a world of good as well. I track my sleep and water intake with various tools. Sometimes, the simple reminder to hydrate and rest is all I need for the world to become right again.

Robin Sharma has a great program called the 5am Club. He suggests that you start every day with some exercise, journaling, and meditation. In my experience, this advice is absolutely on point. It's too rigid for me now that I have small children and so many moving variables in my life. But I did it regularly when I was single and really needed some life shifting and found it to be a powerful combination to create clarity and momentum. I like to be a little more creative with it nowadays, and I sprinkle it into my day where I can. At times, exercise is my moving meditation, and taking a long walk with the dog can also scratch that itch. I allow it to be fluid and ever-evolving, like my diet. I like to check in regularly and let my intuition guide me. I also have decades of regimented practice, so I have found that having more fluidity is beneficial.

Mental Resilience

Speaking of mind management… Getting into an icy pool at 5am when I was 9 years old was a practice of mental resilience, that's for sure! I would focus on how good I was going to feel after the warm-up and how much closer I would be to my goals. Music is another great way to immediately impact your state. A happy or energizing song can get you into the perfect state, something I use all the time as a swimmer. I repeat lines of songs that are empowering as I swim, which started when I was a kid. It was my mantra of sorts before I knew what mantras were. I always had a lot on my plate between swimming and school, and helping my mom at her business or working my own job in the summer as a lifeguard. The full plate taught me time management and further levels of discipline. I found it to be very interesting that when I had less on my plate, I was less efficient. The more robust my schedule, the more I was able to accomplish. And it still rings true for me to this day.

Little actions over time establish habits, and those habits cultivate the soil of our character. The goal is to ensure that our character and core values align with our identity. This whole concept is flushed out beautifully in the book, <u>Atomic Habits</u> by James Clear. It's why making your bed is an important way to start your day as it provides you with a successful completed action first thing upon waking. Having the responsibility of feeding the dog and taking out the trash can give a sense of purpose, as silly as that may sound. These small actions may start simple but over time, they become the fertilizer for the soil that is your confidence and success.

I wrote an article for Invictus Fitness many years ago about the importance of growing your own garden; the critical aspects of self-management and content-ment can be illustrated in the simplicity of a garden. When you first start a garden, you must decide why you want to grow a garden in the first place. Is it for nourishment? Is it for personal enjoyment, esthetics? Why or what are the core values for starting the garden? I think of this as the sun shining down on the garden and allowing it all to flourish. The core values, your why, like the sun, doesn't change much over a lifetime. They may have different expressions, like the way the weather changes, but the essence stays the same.

The soil is made up of habits. The quality of your habits either enrich or deplete the soil you have nour-ishing your garden. Goal setting, meditation, nutrition, exercise, journaling… these are all elements to enrich the soil of your soul. These habits nurture the plant which is the identity or outcome that we seek. The outcome could be flowers, fruits or vegetables, or whatever creative pursuit you can imagine. I see the weather as mind management or our emotions. If the sky is always cloudy, the crop may suffer. If it is always blazing hot, the crop may equally suffer. If the weather is not extreme, but is instead reflective of the appropriate seasons, the crop will flourish. The sun will shine as one stays true to their core values and why (intention), and the weather will pass without significant impact to the crops.

Failure is also beautiful fertilizer for the soil. Hopefully, our failures are a result of taking risks or pushing ourselves in an uncomfortable way. Regardless, there's no doubt that within that failure there was inevitably some degree of success. Reflect on the positive aspects, and grow that success. Equally, evaluate the aspects of the failure and determine what can be modified to yield a different result - and then get back out there and go again.

When you come back to your why, you will cultivate the garden that serves you. "Comparison is the thief of joy," after all. If I am constantly comparing my garden to my neighbors, I might feel less than. If they are growing a garden of flowers and it's aesthetically appealing, how can I compare that to my robust garden of fruits and vegetables that is sustaining my family? Why would I want to compare it in the first place?

That is what we are doing all the time when we go on social media and allow someone's success to make us feel like we are not enough or less than. I have no idea what that person's goals, identity or level of fulfillment is like. I can feel much more at peace if I admire my neighbors garden and congratulate them for their success. Then I come back to my habits and identity and continue to nourish my garden. Then my neighbor has a bounty of flowers to share with me and I have a bounty of fruit and vegetables to share with them. A swimming analogy would be to *stay in your own lane* and *manage the pace that works for you.* It's nice to have a companion to stretch and challenge you but ultimately, you must know what you're capable of as an athlete. We see it all the time when an athlete runs someone else's race and goes out too fast or too slow and doesn't end up achieving their full potential. Comparison is lethal. Celebrating ourselves and others for the effort, achievements, and 'failures' is invigorating.

If I stay true to my core values, my why, and identity I have a much greater likelihood for contentment. I can practice my daily habits of gratitude, journaling, meditation and service to others and my contentment bucket will overflow. So ask yourself, *what is authentic to me and am I living in my most authentic space? Am I focusing on someone else and jealous of their success? If so, what is it in me that is not feeling expressed or fulfilled?* Take the time to sit in silence and ask yourself questions like this regularly. Start to trust the first thing that comes to mind for yourself, and commit to non-judgement. Write these things down on a piece of paper and contemplate your answers. More often than not, the answers you seek are right inside of you. And if not inside of you, you might find it on a billboard or a street sign later that day. Stay open, stay curious. The universe is conspiring for you constantly, but it requires being in a space of openness to receive the information. If you are rushed or distracted, it is likely that you will miss it.

PAUSE: Let's take a mental break together.

This is an exercise I like to do and share with my clients. It's a short meditation which starts off with a progressive relaxation where you imagine softening and

129

letting go from the top of your head to the tips of your toes. Once your physical body has relaxed, imagine a softening of your thoughts. Let your thoughts just float by like clouds in the sky. Remain unattached. Then imagine an emptying of your vessel. Imagine everything you know, believe, and have experienced up to this point, emptying. Like you are a vase dumping its entire contents. Enjoy this space for as long as you'd like. Then, be open to receiving your breath as if it's the first time you are taking it in. Imagine that you are open and available to receive whatever is provided to you as you go about your day. Drink it all in with grace and gratitude. Once you have that intention set, you can gently open your eyes and reconnect with your surroundings.

Deep breathe in… now let it all out.

If my cup is too full and overflowing, I am unavailable to new opportunities and new ideas. I am also less open to listen and hear what's being offered around me. The practice of regularly emptying helps me to destress, unload and cultivate an intention of receiving. So give it a try!

My 'why' is that, by being of service, I come home to myself and can mirror the unlimited potential in myself for others. My core value is growth. If I am serving and growing, I am fulfilled. It's been a thread throughout my whole life. I have always sought adventure, challenge, and learning, and I am the happiest when I can help others in any capacity. When I was young, I wanted to help my mom. Then, in the military, I got to help and encourage the people I worked with. Now, I get to do it as a mom and an alternative healthcare provider. Writing this book is stretching me in a massive way of growth as well and I hope that it serves my children and whomever else reads it however it's meant to.

I consciously align with my why every day by journaling, meditating (usually just for 5 minutes), and reading. I don't always get to read for long periods of time either, sometimes it's just 10 or 15 minutes. But I acknowledge something that I learn every day in a journal. I also surround myself with incredible people. There is the saying that you are the culmination of the 5 people you spend the most time with. I am extremely fortunate for the individuals I have met and get to interact with daily. My husband is an amazing example. He has taught me that words have meaning. He is patient and grounded. He absolutely makes me want to be a better person and my family unit is so beautifully balanced with him as my co-pilot. He helps support me in my authenticity. He encourages me to make myself a priority when I get off course and out of balance. He is, undeniably, one of my greatest gifts.

SQUIRREL!

There are so many distractions available today. When I was growing up it was TV, alcohol, cigarettes and drugs. Now, there is the internet and social media; an unlimited playground of distractions. Social media triggers all sorts of feelings of unworthiness, comparison, and the fear of missing out (FOMO), just to name just a few. Women fall prey to this easily because we are such emotional creatures. We are the storytellers and the town gossip. It makes sense that this medium of communication would draw us in. It's also a very creative medium of self expression. But there are so many ways that social media is used to psychologically manipulate the masses.

If you watch the movie <u>The Social Dilemma,</u> the construct of the algorithms make it seem as if we don't stand a chance against the mind numbing trance and dopamine drip. The algorithms are built to psychologically manipulate us and stay one step ahead. So what's the answer? Do we abandon it altogether? Can it be used for good? I think it can. I think this is where awareness and management of mind becomes so critical, yet again. If it is using us and we are mindlessly scrolling and being triggered, then absolutely, the algorithms win. But if we have restraint and are clear as to exactly what we are using social media for, I believe we can use it responsibly and partake in the enjoyment of it.

We have the power to change the story and to change the narrative, no matter where we've been or what we've experienced. It's an opportunity to spread good news, positive body image, acceptance and unity. It's a space to connect, but not at the detriment of connecting in real time, physically, with real life people. This requires intention when using any medium, but especially social media. It also requires discipline to check the time you're expending on it, and what you are focusing on moment to moment. Taking a break for a week at a time can also be very helpful to evaluate how much time and energy you have actually tied up in the medium, and then you can make a conscious choice as to how you want to re-engage (if you decide to).

A great visual here is imagining a hurricane. In the eye of the hurricane, everything is still. But the hurricane hasn't stopped. There is a wild wind tearing up everything in its path, revolving around the quiet center. I think of awareness like that. Awareness is being in the eye of the hurricane, which can be cultivated through meditation and the practice of being right here and now, over and over again. If you feel yourself getting pulled into the past or the future, take a breath and invite yourself to be present. Do this as many times as you need to recenter and reconnect with yourself, and what matters most. This is how you stay connected to your truth and cultivate deep awareness.

It really does all start with you.

Be The Change

My favorite Gandhi quote is, "Be the change you wish to see in the world." It brings me great peace in a time where it feels like there is so little that I can truly impact. I know I can be the best version of myself possible and I can raise the best humans possible. This is how I will have an impact on the world. I want to be the reason that someone smiles and then for that smile to have a ripple effect out into the world. I hope that my children will exponentiate that ripple effect with their positive actions. It doesn't have to be a huge call to action. Just one step at a time is how all of the greatest structures were built. Just as it is with writing this book; I am accomplishing it one word at a time, one week at a time. Sitting down for a few hours here and there, wherever I make the time to make it happen. And at the end of several months of writing one word, one sentence, one chapter, a full book will be birthed.

Keep it simple. Create a habit. Breathe. Notice your breath regularly. **Your breath is the metronome for your mind,** so start there. Begin to notice when you hold your breath, when you breathe in a shallow manner. Drink plenty of water. If you need a reminder, set your watch to tell you to drink up. Move your body. Play and laugh. Live and be the loving being that you want more of in the world. Soon, that reflection will become your tribe and that ripple effect will spread into the world. It's the best chance we have at making a difference.

I consider myself a very observant individual. The human condition and community fascinate me. As a result, I'm always curious as to how we think, why we think that way, and how much power we have to alter that course. My mom has been the perfect parent for me because if she had done everything the 'optimal' way, I wouldn't have anything to compare or evaluate against. I am certain that I chose her and my dad because they created amazing learning opportunities and psychological experiences for me to consider, and I love them for that. I believe it's experiences such as these that increase human potential.

They prepared me perfectly to do hard things.

Lifeboat Lessons

To bring yourself into the now, try meditation in a few different ways.

1. Take a mango or fruit of your liking and sit quietly for a few minutes. Then take a small bite and imagine you are savoring this fruit for the first

time. Chew very slowly and notice the texture, juiciness, flavor and all aspects of the fruit. Be in the moment of the experience completely. Journal about your experience afterward.

2. Try meditating in a very loud and active place. Can you come to your breath? Are you able to box breath and be in the eye of the hurricane? What was the experience like for you ? Journal about the experience.

CHAPTER 8

The Truth About Confidence

"A flower does not think of competing with the flower next to it. It just blooms." – Zen Shin

Confidence is imperative for success. You can achieve what you believe, and you must have an unwavering belief in yourself to have enduring self-confidence; all of which requires courage. The kind of courage in which you allow yourself permission to choose yourself in every moment, no matter what anyone else thinks or says.

In today's world, with constant (and instant) feedback online, it has become so much more challenging. There is more depression, lack of self-confidence and bullying than ever before. Many people are turning outward for external validation and 'likes' (eh hem, vanity metrics) instead of turning inward to their own conviction in what they believe to be true about and for themselves. And honestly, I don't see this slowing down anytime soon. At least not at the rate we're moving, under our current programming.

Awkward Authenticity

I was a super confident child and I had no issue with being awkwardly authentic. I was reminded of this fact looking back at old pictures of myself at swim meets. Case in point. One of the greatest concerns as a swimmer is having your goggles fall off or fill with water as you enter the water from a dive. Even as recently as the 2021 Olympics, Lydia Jacoby swam the 100 meter breaststroke with her goggles wrapped around her face under her nose. And in 2016, Michael Phelps swam the 200 butterfly with goggles filled with water. It happens to the best in the world. I decided I wasn't going to have that kind of stress or concern messing with my game so I started wearing a goggle cap. It's an alien-like looking contraption where your goggles are built into the swim cap to ensure that they stay securely on your face. Reminiscent of Dumb Donald from Fat Albert. And that's exactly what I looked like.

You can Google the internet for a 'goggle cap' or 'goggles built into a cap' and you will get nothing. That's because they were so ridiculous looking that no one was willing to wear them and look that silly. However, I did not care in the least. I owned one in yellow, pink, green - all the colors that were available. I had a stockpile of these weird headpieces and you know what? My goggles never filled with water and they certainly never fell off of my face. It was one less stress every time I climbed onto the starting blocks and I could care less what anyone else thought of them. I once posted a throwback picture on social media and several of my old swimming buddies got a great laugh out of it. One swimmer, who was several years older than me, even responded saying, "you are 100 percent authentic and always have been." What an epic compliment. I can't imagine if social media had existed back then. I wonder if I would have been impacted by a bunch of unsolicited negative opinions about my appearance. I'd like to think I wouldn't, but it's impossible to know.

Confidently Courageous

It makes sense that people saw me as a leader and a good candidate for the Naval Academy. I didn't have any issue speaking my mind and walking my own authentic walk. I genuinely liked who I was, and had a compelling curiosity of the world around me. I was naturally courageous, maybe a little over confident, and easily led by example. I didn't have as much exposure to the team work aspect, I was used to doing most things on my own, a hard life lesson I had to learn later on. There is no shame in relying on a team to achieve greater success than you're capable of on your own. However, I'd gotten so good at relying on myself throughout my life that my first instinct was often to just dive in without thinking about asking for support. So when a few people challenged me by saying they couldn't see me making it through the Naval Academy, my overconfident-self jumped at the opportunity to prove them wrong.

Plebe summer is the summer training program required of all incoming freshmen to the United States Naval Academy - and it rocked my world. It wasn't the physical demands of the summer, but the stripping away of everything along with having my weaknesses thrown in my face and used against me. But I had a plan. After high school graduation, I went to Spain to spend a few weeks with my sister who was already married and living over there by the beach with her brand new baby. I was supposed to come back to Boise and have a farewell party with my friends before I left for the Academy, but I got hit with a terrible case of chicken pox and had to stay in Spain a few days longer, which meant I would have to fly directly to Annapolis without making a stop home to say goodbye to everyone. Without any family support, I showed up on the first day called Induction Day, and headed into the gauntlet while still recovering from chicken pox. I was supposed to read a booklet called <u>Reef Points</u> so that I could learn all of the military jargon, naval history and traditional songs before arriving. But I was having way too much fun in Spain and then with chicken pox, I never even cracked the book open.

As soon as I arrived we were instructed to strip down to our underwear so we could be outfitted for our uniforms for the summer. People were staring at my pox-littered body and face eager to keep their distance. After our gear was issued we were supposed to run, or 'chop,' through the halls to find our rooms. Not only were we to chop, but we were supposed to run down the center of the hall and when we got to a corner, we were to square the corner with a military pivot and yell "Go Navy, sir!" I rushed into the hallways behind a group of people, hoping there would be safety in numbers. I barely got down my first hallway when a woman yelled in my face, "hit a bulkhead." And I had no idea what she meant. "Hit a what?" "A bulkhead," she screamed back at me. "I'm sorry, but I have no idea what you are saying." She was so flustered with me that she yelled for me to get out of there. If I had read my Reef Points I would have known that a bulkhead is the term for an upright wall of a ship. I was supposed to go to the wall, hit it with my open hand, spin around performing a military about face and yell "ma'am yes ma'am, midhsipman 4th class Fearon." I really should have read that book. I was like Goldie Hawn in Private Benjamin, cluelessly reporting for duty.

Through some miracle, I made it up to my room where there was a girl already there, putting her stuff away. Moments later, we were being yelled at to get into the hallway for more questions and physical exercise. I failed miserably with all of the military knowledge and was required to do extra push-ups and running to make up for my lack of knowledge. That night, I laid in my bed on the top bunk thinking, 'what the hell have I gotten myself into?!' I was all alone, cut off from any familiar lifelines, and grossly unprepared.

The next day, after a run, my squad leader used me as an example of toughness. He pulled one of our company mates aside and berated him for not keeping up. He told him that he should be humiliated that he was being out performed by a girl with chicken pox. The words he used against my classmate didn't make me feel good. It was a backhanded compliment used to degrade one of my classmates. The idea of using chicken pox as an excuse to not try as hard or show up as my best never entered my mind. I gave it my full effort and I knew that, even if I was a little under the weather, my full effort was better than average. I firmly believe that we can all do hard things when we want. Often, it simply requires our commitment to continue putting one foot in front of the other without worrying where we are going or where we have been. Chicken pox or not, I was a hard-worker with an innate drive to succeed. And I have no doubt that my classmate had at least a bit of that within him too, or he wouldn't have signed up for the academy in the first place.

Focused

When I raced the 1650 in swimming, I dove off the blocks and didn't focus on completing 66 lengths of the pool. I tackled it 4 lengths at a time (sometimes just one length at a time, if I was feeling rough) and before I knew it, I would make it to 66. When I raced the Ironman, I took it one mile at a time. During the marathon, I thought about how much I loved going for 5 mile runs and focused on taking it 5 miles at a time. It takes courage to take the first step, but the more steps you take, the easier it gets. And when you realize all the steps that are now behind you, which got you to this very time and place, your confidence in what you're capable of achieving soars. The hardest part in anything you do is starting. Even now, when I go to swim in the ocean, it's the first 500 meters that are the most dreaded and then I am blissed out. Have you ever noticed that some days, you feel so sure that you are going to struggle or have a bad performance and then, you end up having one of the greatest sessions or experiences of your life? All the doubt is just fear. Acknowledge it, then ask it to move over and move on.

I was told so many times in my life that I *could not* or *should not* do things. The first time I can remember having my own will questioned was when I showed up on the pool deck as a kid. I was told I was too small to be a good swimmer and was assured that I would have greater success as a diver. But in my heart, I knew that simply was not true. Then, I was told I would never make it at the Naval Academy. And as much as I wanted to prove people wrong, I also knew I was totally capable of, and up for, the challenge. I wanted stability and structure so badly that I'd committed to doing whatever it took. My motto in life was, 'how hard can it be?' I mean, if someone else had already done it, it certainly wasn't impossible. My favorite Winnie the Pooh quote is, "they say nothing is impossible, but I do nothing all day." Touché, Pooh.

I struggled academically my first year at the Naval Academy. I had a terrible GPA and even had to go to the academic board, which threatened my expulsion. That summer, there was an option to do a sailing cruise as one of our assigned summer blocks. Being on a sailboat in the open ocean sounded much more appealing than a cruise on one of the Academy's small frigate-like ships. The problem was that it was assigned based on academic achievements. Instead of being deterred, I signed up for the sailing cruise. The worst they could do was say no. Which they didn't. I got on the cruise, despite my grades and the rules. And while it may have been a mistake and I have no idea how they said yes, my belief that it was possible worked in my favor through the courageous action to go for it, despite the possibility that I could be turned down.

You see, if you don't ask for what you want, you'll never get it. This applied again when I became an active duty officer and I asked to be the Supply Officer at a SEAL Team. I was cautioned heavily on taking the job and told it would be a neutral mark on my record and had the potential to negatively affect my advancement. But I really wanted the job! I knew if I was doing something that I thoroughly enjoyed and felt like I was making a difference, I would be great at it so I took it, despite the warnings. I learned early on that when I listened to my heart, really incredible things happened. And I believe that's possible for us all, it just takes a bit of practice and a whole lot of courage. Taking that first step makes all the difference.

Heart Speak

It's interesting, the whole, listening to your heart, thing. It's been a real theme throughout my life. And the amazing thing is that there is an innate knowing within each of us, we've just got to lean in and tune in to hear its whispers. When we align with our inner knowing and trust in its ability to support our deepest desires and highest level, we enter a flow state as the universe magically unfolds in front of us. I felt it and I danced with it often, but I wasn't always clear or confident in what came through.

When I started Acupuncture school, Claire introduced me to an amazing German clairvoyant who did readings and past life regressions. I was open to any experience that might teach me more about myself and how I could tap into more of my potential so when presented, I gave it an enthusiastic YES. And I remember the session very clearly.

As I sat across from her in a comfy chair, she brought me into a relaxed state by counting backwards from 10. She then guided me through a meditation where I traveled back through a tunnel. She then had me imagine putting my feet down and then describe what I saw. I did this several times and I remember thinking, 'ah man, I am terrible at this... I am not sure I am seeing or feeling anything!'

I felt like I was lost on a mountain top that looked like the Alps. I felt alone and abandoned, but I wasn't certain what was real or just in my imagination. She had me go back and put my feet down two more times and then it happened - wham! All of a sudden, I was floating over the planet, looking down on all of humanity. Through my curious eyes, I felt a feeling of fear penetrate me as I declared that there was no way I was going back down there. Earth, from my point of view, was not safe. It became abundantly clear to me that something bad had happened down there at some point, all because I had followed my heart. From what I could tell, I had tried to help someone and I was harmed as a result of following my truth. Then I saw my mom's face and chose to push my fear aside so I could come back and try the whole 'human thing' again.

I came out of that session with my mind blown, armed with so much clarity. I had a deep rooted belief that it could be dangerous to follow my heart, yet the desire within me to do just that was so strong it was as if there was no choice at all... it was just what had to be done. I continued to lean into this practice of self-trust time and time again. And while there have been moments I still want to shrink to stay safe, I find myself going inward to the truth of my soul, knowing that I will be okay, and that all is well in my world.

Mind Mastery

My mom encouraged me to have experiences that she was denied; she wanted me to have a better life than she had experienced. She never pushed me in the pool, but she was very encouraging and excited about my opportunity at the Naval Academy and often mentioned how she wished she could have had that experience; the security and simultaneous adventure really spoke to her soul.

When I graduated from the Naval Academy and expressed my disinterest in continuing much farther with the military, she didn't understand. It was clear that she was initially really disappointed in my decision and confused as to why I would give up such an awesome opportunity for a solid retirement. My mom didn't live vicariously through me, but she strongly directed me in a way that she thought was best based on what she couldn't have. It was subtle. But I definitely knew what made her proud and happy. The people-pleaser part of me was so conditioned to appease others (my mom, in particular) that oftentimes, I didn't even see my choices as mine to make. It wasn't until I was further removed from it all that I could see clearly how conflicted I was in truly knowing what I wanted versus it being 'the right thing to do,' like finding structure, security and stability in something worthy, such as the military.

I firmly believe that every human is capable of more than they think. But so often, the mind gets in the way, consumed by self-doubt and fear. Confidence gets rattled by our own negative self-talk or getting caught up in the trap of comparison. That's also where my eating disorder entered. Instead of staying true to myself and honoring what was working for me, I focused on outward appearances, comparing myself to others instead of looking in the mirror with pride, literally, at how strong my body was and how much it did for me every single day. The record played on repeat in my head... *Maybe if I had lost a little weight and was smaller like my competitors I would set more records... Maybe if I was leaner like some of my girlfriends, I would be more attractive.* Comparison is not only the thief of joy, it is the shrouding of our truth. In comparison, we make choices based on someone else's blueprint, which limits finding our own truth and potential for higher levels of authenticity and greatness. How could I be confident in any action if it wasn't coming from an authentic space? By giving my compass away, I was capping my ability to break those glass ceilings and pave a new way - *my way.*

Nowadays when this happens, I go back to the garden analogy and read the quote that I opened this chapter with. I remind myself that if I choose to compare myself to someone else, I am limiting my unique (and important) potential. Besides, thinking of myself as a once-in-a-lifetime expression of unprecedented stardust, I have also come to rely on gratitude. Gratitude invites in the vibration of love and in the space of love, acceptance unfolds. This powerful ripple effect allows comparison to fall away and I am reminded of who I am and why I am here as… *me!* Limitations do not exist in this place, and that is where I choose to live and create from. We must become masters of our mind in order to consciously choose this space over and over again, no matter what lies in front of us. Hard times happen, but we are all strong enough to overcome them.

Missing Pieces

The missing piece in my confidence was love; self-love in particular. I was confident in my ability to do just about anything. I was always ready and willing to prove anyone wrong, and to prove my self-worth to everyone around me while hopefully convincing myself that I was worthy as I was in the process. But everything I had focused on was all about *doing* when really, what I actually needed was to slow the heck down and BE - no action necessary.

Being centered in a space of gratitude and self love, I saw just how skewed my personal view of myself was. When I look back at pictures of myself now I think, 'Wow! I was so pretty, happy and fit!' At the time, though, I struggled to see that; my internal critic usually found something to pick apart. From as far back as I can recall, I struggled with having my picture taken. I had a knack for scanning the picture and finding something that could be better. *What is enough? When will it ever be enough?* Even now, as an adult, I still have moments where I struggle with that. Having two beautiful girls has helped a lot. I see how perfect and amazing they are and I reflect that back to myself. Whenever my oldest daughter is being a perfectionist, I see myself being critical and I do my best to help her work it out. In doing so, I give myself permission to let go and just surrender.

Self affirmations help as well. I'll write words or phrases and post them on my bathroom mirror or by my office desk. Sometimes I write a word on my hand or wrist. *Right now, right here. Everything is unfolding exactly the way it's supposed to and I am exactly where I am supposed to be at this moment right now.* That is one of my favorite mantras. Getting into a space of gratitude and walking my way back to love always softens my critical mind.

I created an awesome meditation where I visualize myself going through every part of my body in awe as if I'm seeing it for the first time, and recognizing the masterpiece in it all. For example, I'll witness my heart and the ventricles pumping as the blood moves through my body, just as my heart and lungs work together to sustain my life. It's like I'm looking at the statue of David or a Monet painting for the first time. I witness my insides as a masterpiece; a living, breathing miracle all the way to the atomic level. By the end of my meditation, after seeing each cell of my body in such a glorified space, I can't help but love myself deeper. It's a delicious practice that I recommend often to my patients. Writing this now, I am reminded to practice it more frequently because it really creates a juicy vibe.

Resiliency of Spirit

Being in the flow of love and gratitude is great therapy. However, life is not easy. Honestly, it can be hard and feel extremely unfair at times. That was starkly evident when I assisted in the Oncology Department at Children's Hospital in San Diego, CA. I'll never forget a little 10 year old girl that was a few weeks from her final days. Someone had given her a copy of the infamous book, <u>The Secret</u>. She was reading the book when I arrived one afternoon and she looked up at me and asked me a painful question. "In this book it says that everything that is happening to me I asked for in some way. It says I created everything in my life. How did I ask for bone cancer?" My eyes welled with tears and I wanted to throw the book across the room and punch the person that gave it to her all at the same time.

"Ah love, I'm so sorry you had to read that today. We humans are doing the best that we can to make sense of this world. We want to feel like we have control so that way we can feel safe and secure. We are flawed and often wrong. The reality is that we don't control much of anything at all. So much of what happens in this world we can't explain. What is happening to you right now is one of those things we cannot explain. You did nothing to ask for this challenge and I am so sorry you have to bear it. I can tell you that through this challenge you have been a gift to everyone that has had the honor to know you. Your presence fills up this room with light and you have deeply touched the lives of each person you meet. You will be in my heart forever." And so she is.

She met everyday with a smile and a great attitude. She often lifted up her parents and assured us all that she was okay. We have so little control and we have no idea how much precious time we get on this planet. While we do have control over our attitude and have the ability to create fierce intentions and manifest our dreams, sometimes shit just happens and there is no way to make any sense of it. This will happen in some way, to some extent, in every person's life. That is why resilience matters so much. The ability to get up, no matter how many times we are knocked down, that's the power of the human spirit.

Resilience is not only critical in the tough times, it's necessary in the good times as well. How many stories have we heard about how the most successful people in the world were told no over and over again? It's true in nature, too. In order for the seed to become a flower, it has to fight and push through the soil, sometimes coming face to face with rocks and even pavement to find its way to the light. But the seed knows no quit, for it's clear that it is here to be more; to bloom into a flower.

The more uncomfortable situations I endure, the more I realize it's all just a sensation and it's up to me to define the sensation. I can call it pain, suffering, even unbearable. Or I can just meet it and be present for the experience, remaining open to whatever is supposed to come through. I don't even have to call it anything, I can just be with the sensation from a place of curiosity and wonder. I think it's important to experience what many would consider *discomfort,* regularly. It's how you build fortitude and resilience. I have personally experienced discomfort many times.

Whether it be long hikes in the Himalayas, getting through my years at the Naval Academy or racing in some of the multi-day adventure races, paired with the discomfort often comes a sense of accomplishment and pride. And it doesn't have to be extreme!

Discomfort can come in stillness, as you sit in silence with yourself for a period of time, bearing witness to your breath and your thoughts. It may come in the form of taking an ice bath, or a sauna as you cultivate awareness of mind and body, and how you manage each thought. Say yes to a public speaking engagement, take an ice cold shower, sing for a group of people, or write a book! The more you can put yourself in uncomfortable situations and see that yes, you absolutely CAN persevere, the more resilient you will become. You will see that you are not your thoughts. And no matter what anyone says, or what you have believed to be true in the past... always remember that you can do whatever your heart desires and you are always more than enough.

Lifeboat Lessons

1. Draw a flower with as many petals as you need to describe your unique attributes. In each petal, write an attribute that you appreciate about yourself. Decorate the flower as creatively as you want. You can add magazine quotes or pictures that remind you of these qualities. Then hang it somewhere that you can see it daily.

2. If you are struggling to come up with all of your amazing attributes, ask 5 of your closest friends

to use adjectives to describe unique qualities about you. Another way to ask for clarification of these things is, *what shows up when you show up? When you enter a room, what is uniquely present?*

CHAPTER 9

Follow Your Weird

"There is a vitality, a life force, an energy, a quickening that is translated through you into action, and because there is only one of you in all of time, this expression is unique. And if you block it, it will never exist through any other medium and it will be lost. The world will not have it. It is not your business to determine how good it is nor how valuable, nor it compares with other expressions. It is your business to keep it yours. Clearly, and directly, to keep the channel open." – Martha Graham

Your weirdness is your superpower. It is your unique blueprint. Martin Luther King, Gandhi, Mother Teresa - they did not create a lasting impact on humanity by following the pack. These leaders had the courage to follow their unique thoughts, ideas and beliefs; they didn't ask for approval or validation to do so. They knew themselves deeply, and acted accordingly. Sometimes, following your own path might feel like swimming upstream against the current. It might even feel like you are swimming upstream against the current while you watch your fellow school of fish cruise downstream, trying to convince you to join them. That's kind of what it felt like when I decided to leave the military and go to Acupuncture school. It was such a stark contrast to what anyone I worked with understood and I was often asked why I wasn't going to pursue something more established or reputable like medical school, which had credibility and clout. I felt the reality of that pressure. Quite a lot, actually.

I explored a bunch of conventional routes before deciding on acupuncture. But none seemed to offer the creative freedom to explore my talents in the way I desired. I took the time to interview several people in the different medical fields beforehand, and often the story I heard was that they felt their hands were tied by the organization and insurance requirements where they worked. Collaborating with a person through their healing process is a dynamic, fluid and somewhat creative process. I had experienced this through my own recent injuries so I knew the power that collaborative care held. There were both physical layers and emotional layers to uncover and repair. I knew I wanted to be a part of a person's healing journey that resulted in a place of empowerment and facilitated a deeper connection with themselves, which to me encompassed many modalities including: yoga, meditation, acupuncture, herbology, visualization, massage therapy, healing touch. I wanted to incorporate all that I had learned, and it was not going to be possible within the confines of conventional medicine. The traditional route left me uninspired and if chosen would once again have me accommodating others. I would be forcing myself to fit in and at that point the thought felt like willingly throwing on a straight jacket. I knew within myself that I had to do it differently, and I could not wait any longer.

Full Body Fuck Yes

Most people back in 2005 didn't even really know what the practice of acupuncture involved. When I told my Executive Officer, he thought I was giving up my promising career to work in some Asian Spa that would offer sexual favors at the close of a session. That conversation gave me a glimpse into his life that would have been better kept to himself. Other mentors of mine convinced themselves that I was going to Physical Therapy School. They still to this day introduce me as a Physical Therapist on occasion. It cracks me up and I don't mind. That is what they can relate to and find acceptable, so I just go with it. My mom loved receiving massages and acupuncture, but she certainly viewed this pursuit as a step down from my military occupation. My siblings are all extremely successful. They work in corporate settings and have fancy titles and impressive connections. I don't think they really knew what a career in acupuncture was going to look like or what exactly I was going to be doing, they just thought giving up my promising military career seemed like a very odd choice. If it's not broken, why fix it? I can totally appreciate that, but from my point of view, it *was* broken. I knew myself and I wasn't happy.

It certainly wasn't an easy time for me and I would be lying through my teeth if I said I was waking up each morning chipper and confident in my decision.

My soul knew I was making the right and best decision for my ultimate happiness and purpose, but my mind still struggled with feelings of doubt and uncertainty as to the road ahead. My stomach was tied in knots and my concerns mounted as I thought about the reality of letting go of the stability, financial security and predictability of a military career and all it affords. I felt like a tightrope walker without a net. I knew I could do it, but it was still scary as hell.

When I think back to the aspects of my life where things actually turned out better than I expected, it's clear that my life has absolutely followed the belief that when one door closes, a better one opens. When thoughts of being homeless and having nothing crept into my mind, I gave myself pep talks which often consisted of me saying something like, "Girlfriend, look at all the hard things you have crushed in your life; this is going to be another one of those things. Now pull up those socks, take a deep breath and walk your ass across that rope. You don't need a net when the universe has got your back." Preach.

Another interesting point about transition is that I always feel like there's some kind of test that accompanies newness. The universe has an amazing sense of humor and truly is conspiring for you, but it will test your conviction as well. Mark. My. Words.

At the exact time that I was getting out of the military to start Acupuncture school, Starbucks wanted to bring its products aboard Navy vessels, which was huge. It made sense that a Supply Officer would be involved in assisting this process and partnership because we understand Supply Chain management and how products are used aboard Navy Ships and on land at the Navy Exchanges. Not to mention, handling contracts and the special ins and outs of working with the military in general. My Commanding Officer at the time approached me and asked me if I had any interest in sitting in on a meeting or being a part of this upcoming partnership. I would be involved as a civilian consultant and the salary would likely be much more than what I was currently making in the Navy. It was an incredible opportunity. I mean, I could do that for a couple of years and then go to acupuncture school, I thought. It was too good an opportunity to say no. So I decided to sit with it for 48 hours. I got quiet and asked my heart, "is this what I want?" And no surprise, the answer was a resounding *no*.

The tempting opportunity was nothing more than a diversion. It was not about the money, it was about the *fulfillment*. I knew I had a gift and I had to pursue that gift, which remaining tethered to the military would not allow me to do. I was going to learn, embody the learning, and pay it forward to empower the people I was blessed to touch with those gifts. The message came through strongly, and it was powerfully clear. Maybe the universe wasn't testing me, maybe it was giving me an opportunity to show up fully embodied in who I knew I was and say yes to myself *fully* this time.

Now as I write this, 12 years into practice, the message has become more crystalized and I know without a doubt that I made the right decision for myself. People come to me for so much more than healing needles to support meridians or clear musculoskeletal blocks. They are showing up for the experience and the magic that happens on the table in my treatment room. Massage, yoga, acupuncture, energy work and meditation are just tools to help people return to homeostasis and balance the system. Sometimes that can happen with a hug or just being heard on a deeper level. There are so many windows for healing.

When the system is balanced physically, mentally and emotionally, there is a greater opening for healing to occur. We have so many resources within our body to heal ourselves and bring us back online to a balanced state. In the process of realigning, people are invited to establish an intimate relationship with themselves and to live their most fulfilling life possible. This book is my invitation to you to deepen your own innate knowing of yourself and step into the fullness of the life waiting for you to be brave.

Pause, be present, and ponder who you really are and what you want out of this brief life we're all so fortunate to experience. We are here on this planet for merely a blip in time. How can you make the most out of it and suck the juice out of every precious second?

Layers of the Journey Home

I have been so honored to witness the transition of some of my most beloved beings as they make their journey onward to the other side. I have been equally honored to witness the ushering in of new beings. I get to participate in anywhere from 2-3 births a year in a support role for clients or friends of mine. It is in these experiences that what really matters becomes shockingly distinct. Unconditional love permeates the room and the presence of God is palpable. My soul feels a validation that our relationships, memories and experiences with one another are our most valuable possessions. These moments crystalize that awareness that nothing else matters. There is no thought of what's been accomplished, the amount of money or accolades earned, or the question of *did I do enough?* All I have ever felt is gratitude for those deep and meaningful connections, along with a profound sense of love.

When Claire passed away I remember being so grateful for all of the special memories we created in such a short amount of time. I always made the time to connect and be present with her, just as she did for me. The last few weeks of her life I dedicated myself to being with her and letting her know how much she meant to me and how much I loved her. And when my sweet friend, Mariel had me over to share some terrible news with me in 2018, I was right there to bear witness and be a participant in her journey as well.

After a trip to visit her son, Mariel had some digestive distress so she went to the doctor. It was there that she discovered that she had stomach cancer, and was given just a year to live. Once again I was utterly devastated. I left her house that day and sat in my car sobbing so hard I thought I was going to vomit. I literally couldn't breathe. She had been there to help me grieve Claire and now she was asking me to help her transition to the other side. Of course my answer was yes, but I couldn't stop crying. It felt impossibly cruel and unfair. Every night for weeks, I would go do healing touch with her to feel her spirit and let her know that she would live forever in my heart. It wasn't goodbye with either of them, it was *until later.* I know Mariel wanted me to be by her side as she transitioned because I provided a sense of comfort and peace. I helped her feel like everything was going to be alright and felt honored to have been able to hold her hand as she transitioned into the unknown. It was also deeply painful to let go of another soul sister.

Mariel saw the cosmic magic at play behind the scenes of life and held my hand when I ventured down some of the darker, scarier paths. She always held up her light and assured me there was perfection in all of the unfolding, reminding me to trust. It was my turn to return the favor and assure her that it was okay, to let go, and that all was well. It really is such an honor to hold such sacred space of unconditional love for those transitioning into or out of this world. Selfishly, that energy feels absolutely glorious to bathe in and oddly enough, it doesn't scare me. But none of that diminished the crushing pain of losing her. I am grateful to provide such a sense of peace and safety for people going through those spaces who tend to find me right when they need me. Especially those I care for deeply.

I have a huge stack of Mariel's books in my office. I often pull one and ask her for her support and she's always there to show me the way. Her husband gave me her collection of swim caps and goggles as well so I feel her when I suit up to head into the ocean. I miss her like crazy but I know she's always with me, and there's comfort in that.

My dad passed away in January of 2019 and fortunately, I was able to sit with him during his last 5 days of life as well. By the time I arrived in Bangor, Maine, he was unable to talk. The doctors told me that they doubted he recognized me, but I knew my dad and I was certain that he felt my presence. He was septic and they were asking me what I wanted to do because my dad hadn't prepared anything. I knew my dad would not want to have his life dragged out in any sort of undignified way. They had to wrap up his hand in gauze and tape like boxing mitts because even in his weakened state, he was trying to pull out his tubes and get the hell out of there. A fighter to the end.

When it became evident that his organs were shutting down, they asked me if I wanted to move him to the hospice floor and let him go peacefully. I had no doubt in my mind that it was absolutely what he would have wanted. I sat with him and talked and although he had no words to share with me, and no movement in his body other than occasionally flailing his arms when he became agitated, I could feel him and that's what mattered.

Our souls had some really beautiful talks during his last days. I thanked him for all of the qualities that he had given to me that allowed me to be such a determined and resilient being. I told him about how some of that DNA clearly made it into my girls and that parts of him were going to live on forever. I forgave him and began to understand him better in those 5 short days than I had in all of our days prior. It was one of the most painful and amazing experiences of my life. I felt moments of regret that it had come to this in order to find peace and closure in our relationship. But then I found a sense of peace as I accepted that this was the way it was meant to be. Beautifully, so much healing and grace transpired without a single word from him. I was playing The Long Time Sun by Snatam Kaur, one of my most favorite songs, and I fell asleep for 5 minutes after midnight just as he took his final breath. He waited until I was asleep to sneak away.

My dad had always wanted to live out in the woods with his dog enjoying the simplicity of life in Maine. Throughout his life he had experienced periods of accolades, money and all the trappings of a successful life. But in the end, it was the simple life that he wanted more than anything. He left the small town of Brownville Junction, where he had made a really impressive life considering all he was up against. He brought many of the people he grew up with along for the ride and they all flourished as a result. But he was crazy stubborn and as such, he died mostly alone. He followed his weird to an extent, but cared way too much about what everyone thought and wanted so much to be admired for his accomplishments and success that he got lost in the pursuits. I hope he knew I admired him. And I hope he found peace as he passed knowing how loved he was.

The Stuff is Shit

Here's the thing. So much of the stuff we end up focusing on doesn't matter. Instead, it becomes a distraction from the essence of what really fills our cup. The house, the car, the stuff... none of that will keep you fulfilled long-term. As a nation, we have more stuff and do more stuff than most other countries, yet we are a country with increasing levels of illness, suicide and depression. We are chasing the external instead of taking the time to come home to ourselves and really know who we are and what has deep and profound meaning to us. We're worried about how many 'likes' or views some silly post on social media got. People are ignoring personal relationships to gain validation from a cyber community of people - and for what? We've become addicted to the dopamine rush that 'more' provides, and we don't even know why we want it, only that it feels good… albeit temporarily. Meanwhile, the people in our lives that know us and care about us are begging for moments of real connection. Stop hiding in the bathroom checking Instagram and go connect with your kids, your spouse, your friends!

Take the time to turn off the TV and put the cell phone away, and be intentional as you really connect with your loved ones. Hold their hand, rub their feet and talk about how they are feeling and what they are passionate about right now. Asking, *how was your day?* can be a cliché entry point. There's a feigning of interest, but how much patience or desire do you really have to hear the full answer? Asking, *how is your heart?* may be way too touchy-feely for some people at first, but that's the essence of real connection. How can we hear each other and be heard without 'canceling' one another because of a post on social media or a snippet of a video someone caught candidly? It starts within. Know thyself, love thyself, be patient and curious with thyself first. You cannot have those experiences with others if you don't cultivate those same qualities within yourself.

It doesn't take monumental action, it takes consistency. The accumulation of actions over time establishes habits that yield powerful results, relationships included. Committing to just 5 minutes of meditation each day has the power to set the tone for your day and your week more powerfully than meditating for 1 hour a week. Give yourself an hour, or even 30 minutes in the morning, to focus and set your intentions before you look at your phone or check your email. Kiss your loved ones and connect with them before you allow yourself to connect with technology. Your actions speak louder than your words so if the phone has a greater priority than the loved ones around you, they will feel it. Make it a practice to be fully present with your loved ones every day. Sit with them and give them your full attention and notice where your mind goes in the process, without judgement. Have a phone-free zone at meal times so that you can connect with one another. Ask questions and really listen. It may sound simple or obvious but in today's busy world, how many of us really practice this on a regular basis?

Our phones have become an extension of our appendages and our attention spans are ever-dwindling because we are constantly distracted and stimulated by the outside world. It's a challenge for sure, and I struggle with it myself at times. But I can absolutely tell by my kids' behavior and how they react to me when I am out of balance in this area which means, it's time to re-center to re-engage. There is no place for perfection; that's a silly and impossible standard to strive for. My goal continues to be to maintain one foot on the path and not to stray too far away with the other. Sometimes it's just a toe, but then I know it's time to re-evaluate and prioritize differently to come back to what matters, and be present with the people and things I love most.

One of the greatest compliments I have ever received from my patients is being told that, when they are with me, they feel like they have my total attention. It's a great feeling and I love that I am able to hold such a solid container for them during our time together. Because you know what? When someone stops and is fully present with you that, in itself, can have a profound healing effect.

Unfortunately in the medical world, having quality time with your medical provider in a way that they get to know you and can care for you in a comprehensive way can be challenging to come by. I don't fault the doctors; they have an impossible task to keep up with overhead expenses, insurance billing, and malpractice insurance. They cannot afford to spend more time with you and additionally, meet the demands that our medical system places on them. That intentional time with my patients is one of the most rewarding aspects of what I do, bridging the gap for people so they are reminded that they matter and others do care.

Lifeboat Lesson

1. Take some time to consider what your current garden looks like. What do you want in your garden metaphorically? How often will you tend to it? What will be your preferred tools to manage it? Will it be regular meditation, visualization, journaling, regular exercise or some perfect mix of all of it? Who do you want to share your garden with?

Closing

"When we deny our stories, they define us. When we own our stories, we get to write a brave new ending."
— Brené Brown

I love this quote from Brené Brown. She is one of my heroes. I would like to take the liberty to add to that quote and say, we also have the power to own our story, close the book and write a whole new book! You have the choice as to how you will define the way you relate to the stories, and how they impact you moving forward. You get to decide if it's all unfolding exactly the way it's supposed to and if you're in the right place at the right time. Not society. Not anyone else! Make your own magic and count your blessings every day, even if it's just the fact that you woke up and have hot water available.

Since we are having a human experience, in a human body, we have an ego. That ego looks for identification and identification can be used for good to empower ourselves and others. If I identify as a compassionate healer, I will make choices and create habits that support that identity. That can be really fulfilling. I might choose to read articles and take classes that support my success in that area. I will want to walk the talk which means that my nutritional habits and curiosity align by way of healthy choices.

I can also identify as a loving mother and wife with a desire for adventure. I'll make time to be present and connect with my loved ones, and seek out experiences that align with that identity. I can have one identity or a few simultaneously. At one time in my life, I identified as a collegiate swimmer and a military officer. Now, those titles aren't in the forefront of my identity anymore. I think that having identities is part of being human and they can absolutely help us create habits to support our success in those roles. The tricky part comes when we believe that the essence of our acceptance and self-worth is tied to any specific identity. No identity is superior to another the same way no wave is superior to another; they are all part of the ocean. It comes down to what I believe about myself at the core of my being.

My identities all morph over time and serve me and my experiences in life in different ways, at different times. Is being a mom *less than* being a military officer? Heck no! So why would we feel the need to compare them? At the core of my being I am a loving, passionate being that wants to make a difference in the world through service. I can serve as a mom, a healer, a military officer, an athlete, a wife... the list is as long as my imagination can take me. I have to know myself, my values and what fills my cup though in order to fuel my imagination and allow myself to strive for new heights. As I grow, so do my present moment experiences. And I think that's what life's all about - evolution (of self and as a whole), and enjoying the ride!

Same goes for you.

Words to Live By

Don't take yourself too seriously. Life is meant to be FUN. Whenever I get my girls ready to go out the door I tell them we are going on an adventure. I want them to experience the world in that way. Who knows who we may meet on our journey, who we may get to help or who might help us. Let's interact with the world like it's a big exciting adventure waiting to unfold for us. Because it is! Doesn't that sound like a fun way to start your day?

And you might as well start in your own neighborhood. Take a walk and see what and whom you discover. It might be a butterfly drinking from a flower with its proboscis, or maybe you'll bump into your 94 year old neighbor and she'll share a special memory that brings her joy and subsequently, puts a smile on your face as well. Choose to find meaning in your experiences because life really is full of magical moments, and people. Attitude and state create your reality - and you're in charge of both. If you don't like what's going on, it's up to you to change your situation or change your perspective. You can move... you're not a tree!

If you're open to seeing the world through the lens of curiosity and adventure, you'll be more likely to feel like you're in the right place at the right time. How many times have we heard a terrible story of how a day unfolded only to find out that the events were essential to saving someone's life?

As an example, a client of mine got a new dog. She took her dog to the park with a friend that said her dog was really friendly. The two dogs got to playing and it quickly turned bad. She reached in with her hand to rescue her dog and her finger was almost amputated. At that moment, it made sense that she was frustrated and even a bit angry with the dogs and their behavior. For whatever reason, the surgery to repair her finger required a chest x-ray where they discovered something even bigger: lung cancer. Because of that dog fight, they were able to diagnose and treat the cancer quickly, taking some of her lung out just in time to save her life. Thank goodness that dog bit her finger almost clean off! If he had just nicked it, who knows how the story would have ended.

Perspective is everything. Choose wisely.

Loving What Is

The experience of being with my dad when he passed was one of the most powerful moments of closure, empathy and healing in my whole life. I felt his heart and his struggles. Most people are trying to be the best versions of themselves that they can be. He didn't have the kind of mentorship and desire for self-discovery that I do. Vulnerability and self-love weren't noble characteristics in his upbringing. But I know that he did the very best that he could. Forgiveness flowed easily in those sacred moments. I do my best to remember that now with everyone I encounter. Most people are doing the best they can, even if we can't see it. What does it really cost for me to give them grace and empathy? Not a whole lot.

I have had extremely high standards for myself and as a result, I've had a tendency to be pretty judgy at times. The experience with my dad humbled me massively, and softened the edges of my judging nature for which I am so grateful. Practicing forgiveness towards yourself and others regularly will heal you on the deepest levels. There is this beautiful prayer that I use and share frequently with my patients, it's the Ho'oponopono Hawaiian prayer for forgiveness. This prayer is like a mantra and can be used to forgive others or yourself and it's a great practice for self-love. Ho'oponopono roughly translates to "cause things to move back in balance" or "make things right." I recite it when my mind gets away from me to soothe anxiety or when I am struggling in a relationship, or even a business negotiation. You can imagine the person you might be having a challenge with in front of you as you recite the mantra. It's also perfect for when I am being really hard on myself. I'll use this mantra to forgive and accept myself in the moment. Recite the mantra for as many rounds as you need until you feel complete.

This is the prayer: "I'm sorry, please forgive me, thank you, I love you." It's that simple. The final part is the most powerful because you are acknowledging your love for yourself and others. And so it is.

What if when we interacted with someone we tried to see more of the soul of that person instead of the armor they may show up with? What if we gave them the benefit of the doubt and remembered that they want acknowledgement and acceptance just like we do? What if we remembered that they are really giving it the best they've got at that moment? What if we could let them know that they are enough through our presence and extending our heart authentically, without expectations of getting anything in return? I think about that with my family and friends. I try hard to let them know that I see them and I value them. I hope they feel it. I believe they do.

As our world becomes more automated and we expand the AI influence, we risk losing true connection and the experience of the human spirit. Imagine seeing the Louvre through AI. You see the art up close and avoid the crowds. The clarity and experience of the place can feel very real and beautiful, but also very sterile. It takes away the chance encounters that you have with other people along the way.

I think back to getting off the train in Barcelona with my friend and not knowing where we would stay that night. An elderly woman came up to us and asked us if we needed some help and offered a place in her hostel. In that hostel we met a couple of Canadians that took us to a great party and showed us some of the best party spots in Barcelona. If I had experienced Barcelona through AI imagery, none of those rich memories would be part of my reality. I guess some fun scenarios could be programmed in, but the magic and spontaneity of adventure and unique human connection becomes impossible. We don't get to share our stories with one another and develop meaningful connections without being present in real time. We become more like cyborgs and robots as we hand over the x-factor of our lives and program in predictability. I guess it can create a sense of certainty and safety, if that's what you are looking for. But it dampens the light of the humanness we all possess, a pretty incredible thing to experience if you ask me.

Adventure, in a thrill-seeking sense, can still exist through things like AI, but coincidences and magic would have to be programmed in. When this happens, we no longer get to experience the coincidence or magical moments of the universe and I firmly believe that it's those very instances that create the beauty of being on this human plane at this time.

So go for it. Embrace the beauty of the human spirit. Embrace the beauty of all that you are right now - as well as all you have been and will inevitably become. Get to know your spirit, intimately and commit to being WILDLY YOU. You are a precious gift and there's no doubt you were placed here at this time with a divine purpose. You are powerful. You are unique. You have qualities that nobody else could possibly touch (yeah, you're that amazing!). Then pay it forward by encouraging others to do the same. Because when we choose, collectively, to live full out, we will become the most powerful versions of our WILD selves and as such, step into the change we want to see through our authentic and unapologetic becoming.

I see you.

I believe in you.

And I am on this journey right along with you.

Here's to me being WILDLY ME and to you being WILDLY YOU.

Acknowledgements

This book is firstly, dedicated to my girls and my husband. Izzy and Gabby gave me the courage to write this book because I wanted to share with them the mistakes and lessons I have learned along the way in hopes that they might have an appreciation and understanding of their crazy mom. I want these powerful ladies to feel fully supported in discovering their unique gifts, to know that they have a safe place to land and encourage them to challenge themselves often and know that failure is a necessary part of success. I love you two more than you will likely ever comprehend. You are my heart living outside of me and while it's often terrifying, it's mostly exhilarating. I can't wait to see how you impact the world.

Brandon, my soulmate, my rock. I am certain this is not our first lifetime together. There is a familiarity and passion that makes for the most wonderful and enduring love. Without you, none of this would be possible. I am a better person because of how you show up everyday. You challenge me to be more patient and self-loving. You have given me the safest space to be Wildly myself.

Suki, our sweet golden-doodle rounds out our family unit and reminds us all in every moment that unconditional love is real and it can be so easy. She is pure love.

Then to my family. My mom, dad, siblings, and extended family. You have been critical in my developmental experiences, each setting great examples of things I wanted and some choices I tried to avoid. Through every step, you were always there as an honest sounding board.

To my friends. I could write another book about all the remarkable people I have encountered in this life; I am beginning to understand why acceptance speeches are impossible. In reality, it is the culmination of all the lives that have touched us that allow us to fully experience who we really are. You are all incredible! Thank you for loving me even when I'm overcommitted and doing too many things at once. Thank you for loving the real me and not expecting me to show up differently. Thank you for nodding with enthusiasm every time I come up with my next adventure and idea. My tribe is epic! You know exactly who you are.

My teachers and mentors. Thank you for your encouragement. I was once described by a superior as a red corvette that would just take off down the road. He saw it as his job to steer me in the right general direction and make sure I didn't get too far off track. That's a pretty accurate description of working with me. My passion isn't for everyone and my stubborn streak can be tricky. But for those that had the ability to bring out my best, I am forever grateful to you. Please know I'm doing my best to pay it forward.

To my clients who bring so much magic to my life. Thank you. As much as you believe I am helping you heal, you are mirroring the healing back to me. There is the saying that if you want to grow, help others and if you want to help others, sit in silence and work on yourself. My work enables the perfect blend of self reflection and service. I truly have won the lottery in life with the level of service I get to provide and the opportunity for introspection.

For anyone that has walked through my door and been on my table, this book is you. You provided the space for me to see myself more clearly and grow into the healer that I am. Thank you for your trust and openness.

I am profoundly humbled by my life and the wonderful people I have met along the way.

About The Author

Heidi Fearon Barker is a skilled acupuncturist specializing in Orthopedics and maintains additional certifications in Functional Medicine, and various Energy Healing modalities. She has experience with a range of professional athletes from CrossFit, Football, Track and Field, Triathlon and many other sports. She has spoken internationally on Mindset for athletes and co-authored the Invictus Mindset Book. She also creates customized visualizations for her clientele.

Heidi has a unique combination of experience and skills as a retired Naval Commander, former collegiate swimmer and now, Doctorate of Oriental Medicine. She uses her life experience to teach Mindset Mastery to her clients as well as helping them find the root of their physical ailments. She utilizes numerous bodywork modalities, nutritional and hormone balancing therapies, corrective exercises and Mindfulness approaches. She is a true Wellness Coach.

As she invests her time healing and inspiring others, Heidi herself is grounded by the loves of her life: her husband, Brandon and their two beautiful daughters, Isabel and Gabrielle, and their goldendoodle, Suki. She loves traveling, learning, and being active.

You can visit my website at www.heidifearon barker.com.